D1215582

Mala Femina

Mala Femina

A Woman's Life as the Daughter of a Don

Theresa Dalessio
with Patrick W. Picciarelli

BOOKS

Fort Lee, New Jersey

Published by Barricade Books Inc.
185 Bridge Plaza North
Suite 308-A
Fort Lee, NJ 07024
www.barricadebooks.com

Library of Congress Cataloging-in-Publication Data

Dalessio, Theresa.
  Mala femina : a woman's life as the daughter of a Don /
Theresa Dalessio with Patrick W. Picciarelli.
    p. cm.
  Includes index.
  ISBN 1-56980-244-0
  1. Dalessio, Theresa. 2. Mafia--New York (State)--Long
Island. 3. Female offenders--New York (State)--Long Island--
Biography. 4. Criminals--New York (State)--Long Island--
Family relationships. I. Picciarelli, Patrick. II. Title.

HV6452.N72M3428 2003
364.1'06'0974721--dc21
[B]   2003040411

Printed in Canada
First Printing

Contents

Acknowledgments

To Dr. Donatelli who has kept me in this world longer than I expected.

To my friends Ann Cunningham, Ann Fiore, Nancy Tickle, and Nike; we shared so much together.

Much love and appreciation to my family who stuck by me through everything.

To Kim Cory, the best stripper in New York for more than fifteen years, who repeatedly told me, "Your life's a book, why don't you write it?"

Introduction: On the Run

"What the hell were you thinking, Tommy?"

I was livid. The love of my life, Tommy Ernst, had the good sense to hook up with me, but when it came to making business decisions, he lacked the smarts, big time.

Tommy's business was hijacking, stickups, and whatever else could put a person away for life. Normally he took tremendous chances, and occasionally he overstepped his bounds. This had been one of those times.

"Ah, c'mon, Terri," Tommy said, as he waved me off with a well-manicured hand. "Joey and his brother find the truck empty, I'll tell 'em somebody ripped it off between the time I sold 'em the swag and the time they got to it."

"You really think they're gonna believe some junkie just happened to come by a truck loaded with $35,000 worth of Sheetrock and walked away with it?" I was incredulous. "And then leave the fucking truck? What did he do, haul the stuff away on his back?"

7

Tommy was sitting on an overstuffed chair in the living room of our Staten Island home smoking a pipe. His appearance was the exact opposite of what the average citizen thinks a gangster looks like. If I had to label my thirty-four-year-old lover, I'd have to say he resembled a cross between Donald Trump and James Dean, with a penchant for stealing things. He'd spent most of his life as a career criminal.

But now that career was about to come to a screeching halt. He'd charged the Bilotti brothers—made guys with the Gambinos—a lot of money for an imaginary load of hijacked goods. Tommy had ripped off two of the most dangerous men in New York. Never mind that the Bilottis were considered friends of my family, brought into the mob by my Uncle Alex. This was about money, and in the mob, that's where loyalty ends. Forget what you've seen in romanticized Mafia movies; it's all about money. There's no such thing as honor. Your best friend is usually the one that shoots you in the back of the head. Surprise.

"Relax, will ya. I do this shit all the time, you know that," he said.

He did it all the time, all right. He loved to scam people, con the average citizen, and make piles of money. But Joey and Tommy Bilotti weren't average citizens. I knew that as soon as they opened the back of that truck and found it empty, they'd come gunning for Tommy Ernst.

I was worried for Tommy, and I tried to think of a way to help him. My family ran Staten Island for the mob, therefore I had some influence. For fifty years, the Dalessios had been the power behind all the rackets on the island. And I was no shrinking violet. I'd meet the challenge head-on.

Tommy Bilotti would later be gunned down with Paul Castellano in front of Sparks Steak House in Manhattan. But this was 1971, and I had to deal with him and his brother ASAP. If they came after Tommy, they'd have to come through me first.

"I think this time you scammed the wrong people," I said as I walked to the window and pulled the drapes closed.

We waited for the inevitable phone call.

❋ ❋ ❋

The phone rang a little after midnight. It was Joey Bilotti.

Tommy and I were in bed, but we weren't getting much sleep. I picked up the phone on the first ring.

"That asshole boyfriend of yours there, Terri?"

"No." What did he expect me to say?

"I ain't got the time to play hide-and-seek. You tell him we can make this square, but he's gotta meet with me and my brother. We want our fucking money back."

"What money?"

He ignored me.

"You tell him he's gotta meet with us, like right now."

"I'll see if I can find him," I said. Tommy was on the edge of the bed, his head pressed against mine as we shared the receiver.

"Country Club Diner," Bilotti said. "In two hours. There's people there, he's got nothing to sweat. First we talk, okay?" He hung up.

I swung out of bed and went for a cigarette. Tommy jumped up and began fumbling with his pants.

"Where do you think you're going?" I asked.

He looked at me like I had two heads.

"To meet with them. You heard him."

I yanked a shirt out of his hands. "Tommy, they're not there to talk. The least that'll happen is they'll kidnap you, torture you. They want their money. You ripped them off."

Tommy snorted, then smiled. "You don't think I can't bullshit my way out of this? Hey, when I left that truck, it was loaded with Sheetrock, just like I said."

We argued for another ten minutes, but Tommy was so full of himself that he thought he could talk his way out of the jam and still keep the money.

"I'm going with you," I said and shed my nightgown.

This led to another heated debate, which I won. If the meeting was an ambush, I theorized, the Bilottis wouldn't start shooting with the daughter of a mob captain present. If I should get hurt, there'd be hell to pay.

I had the bright idea to park the car a few blocks away from the diner.

"So they don't see the car pull up. I think it's the right thing to do." Tommy agreed. That move wound up saving his life (and possibly mine).

The diner was less than a ten-minute ride away, and we got there a little after 3 AM.

It was a cold March night. The bridge and ferry crowd were filtering inside the diner after a night of partying in "the city." The opening of the Verrazano Bridge a few years earlier had unleashed a whole new generation of Staten Islanders on Manhattan who might otherwise have never made the trip.

The parking lot was jammed with cars. As we neared the entrance, weaving our way through a gaggle of big-haired babes, I saw the interior lights go on in a late-model green Ford on the far side of the lot.

At the same time, another car door opened closer to us. The Bilotti brothers were in the first car, and a giant in a black leather jacket (who looked forty but had to be sixty because it takes years of practice to be that ugly) was getting out of the second.

They had intended to box our car in when we pulled into the lot. We'd taken them by surprise when we strolled right past them.

But now they'd spotted us, and we had to make a decision.

"Tommy," I said, "run!"

"Hey!" the giant yelled.

I heard Joey Bilotti scream, "Hey, Ernst, we got somethin' for ya."

I knew that Tommy had been set up. The Bilottis had no desire to talk, they wanted their revenge, screw the money.

Egress from the parking lot was blocked by the rampaging wops behind us, so we headed straight into the diner.

The place was filled to capacity, most eating steaks and mountains of scrambled eggs. These were the years before the cocaine boom, when people still had appetites, particularly after a night of drinking.

We made no pretense of trying to blend into the crowd. We froze momentarily, contemplating our next move.

"Through the kitchen," Tommy said, grabbing me by the arm. I didn't need much persuading.

We barely raised an eyebrow among the diners as we blasted past them and through the "Out" door of the kitchen, sending a waiter with an armload of dishes careening across the hard floor.

I heard cursing behind me, but couldn't tell if it was the kitchen staff or our pursuers. We blew out the back door like we'd been shot from a cannon, picking up speed after we hit the street, making for our car.

We left the Bilottis waving their fists at us as we peeled away in my red-and-white Eldorado.

❋ ❋ ❋

There were two things I learned from our experience. One: Always wear sensible shoes to a mob sit-down. You never know when the meeting might go bad or turn into an ambush and you have to sprint like Jesse Owens to save your life. And two: The Billotis didn't give a damn if I was Nixon's daughter, let alone the offspring of a made capo. These guys were nuts. If I got in the way of them clipping Tommy Ernst, well, so be it.

We hid out in a motel in Brooklyn for two days. No way to live.

"It's my mess, Terri," Tommy said. "You take off, go home. They're after me, not you."

Tommy Ernst had been a part of my life since I was a teenager. We'd drifted apart, married others, but got back together after thirteen years when our respective marriages fell apart. This was the first time I'd ever seen him scared. He'd finally deduced that none of his glib bullshitting was going to extricate him from the mess he was in this time. But I wasn't about to desert him.

I had an idea.

"I think we should go see my Uncle Mike," I said. Mike was my father's brother and had a big say in the day-to-day running of the family's operations. Besides, he liked Tommy because he was an earner. That was the highest compliment you could pay an associate.

"You think he could straighten this out?" Tommy said, with hope in his voice.

What I wanted to tell him was that we stood a better chance of getting a second fortune cookie in a Chinese takeout joint, but I didn't want to make it sound like a long shot. "You made him more money than all his soldiers put together. He could mediate this thing before it goes any further."

My uncle and Tommy had worked a copper-theft racket for quite a while. Tommy would case a brewery somewhere in the tristate area and clip the lock off the front gate in the middle of the night. He'd replace it with his own lock, go get my uncle and muscle guys he called "googans," and go back to the brewery. They'd let themselves in, relock the gates behind them, and proceed to strip the place of every ounce of copper in the building. They'd have the copper fenced before the morning shift showed up for work.

Tommy loved metal. He also loved to steal. Quite the combination. I remember he'd be sitting around the house for a few days getting antsy because he hadn't stolen anything in a while. He'd jump in the car and cruise the streets looking for the huge wheels of copper wire Con Edison had all over the city. He'd locate several wheels, go out and steal a garbage truck, and visit the wheel sites, scooping up as many as five a day. The thefts got to be so lucrative that he had to buy property on Staten Island just to store it all.

He'd have a crew burn off the protective layer of rubber that was wrapped around the copper wire, and he'd sell the load in New Jersey. Tommy made hundreds of thousands of dollars and shared it with my family as tribute.

Other times he'd say, "I gotta go out and make a

score," and come back later that day with a truck-load of stolen goods or a pile of cash.

Tommy Ernst wasn't the boy next door, but I loved him.

I made the necessary phone call.

"Uncle Mike's at Wild Acres," I said after hanging up. "He said come on out." I looked at my watch. "If we leave now, we can be there in a couple of hours."

Wild Acres was the name my family gave the estate they'd created in the Poconos. About an hour from the George Washington Bridge, the Dalessios had built a mansion on 750 acres of woodlands, near the town of Dingmans Ferry. There's a fifty-car parking lot next to the house, surrounded by a stone wall adorned with statues imported from Italy. The inside amenities included nine bathrooms, all marble-tiled, and more cathedral ceilings than in St. Pat's.

Tommy drove while I watched for a tail. Relieved that no one was following us, we settled in for the ride. Tommy had an M1 carbine jammed under the front seat just in case.

It was early afternoon when we arrived. The house was situated two miles down a dirt road just wide enough for one car. My family liked seclusion. Luckily it hadn't snowed in a while, and the road was clear.

My Caddy broke out of the woods into a clearing, revealing an impressive house, complete with an indoor pool. It had taken three years to build, and my family was always making improvements. A five-car garage was nearing completion.

We pulled to the front of the house via a circular driveway. My Aunt Margie came out before we had a chance to get out of the car. Margie was a rough broad, a buxom German bleached-blonde who reminded me of a Panzer tank commander. I wasn't crazy about her. She wore a tight, low-cut sweater and shorts that were two sizes too small (her uniform of the day) and seemed impervious to the cold.

She jerked a thumb over her shoulder. "He's at the lake." She turned and went back into the house. Miss Personality.

There was a lake on the east end of the property with a small island in the middle. My uncle liked to row the lake for relaxation and fish for the trout he had stocked every season.

"Which way?" Tommy asked.

"It's best we go back the way we came in. I'll show you the cutoff. We'll have to walk. The Caddy's too wide to navigate the trail."

Tommy swung the car down the road. We were about halfway between the main road and the house when I heard an engine rev behind us.

A dirty black Chevy came barreling through a waist-high patch of bushes. Coming right for us.

"Jesus fucking Christ!" Tommy yelled and floored the Caddy.

The chase was on.

We hurled down the dirt road, hitting every bump and rut we'd been so careful to avoid on the way in. A safe top speed on that road couldn't have been more than thirty-five mph. We were doing sixty.

Tommy had the steering wheel in a death grip, his focus straight ahead. Despite the bouncing, or because of it, I was able to turn myself around on the passenger seat. I was now on my knees facing our pursuers.

Tommy took a hard right onto the main road, which was little more than a poorly maintained two-lane secondary highway. He floored the pedal, and I was propelled into the seat, chest first.

"How many are there?" Tommy screamed.

There was some dust kicking up, but through the cloud I saw two figures in the front seat. I automatically assumed it was the Bilotti brothers, but I couldn't be certain.

Our Caddy had the power to outdistance them. We were slowly putting a comfortable space between us as we approached eighty mph.

I began to feel a little relieved.

Tommy jerked his head to the rearview mirror every few seconds. He also seemed to decompress a bit, but kept the speed up.

An arm extended out a window of the Chevy. I saw a muzzle flash before I heard the gunshot.

"They're shooting at us!" I bellowed. Bullets had a perverse way of closing our lead.

Tommy crouched down in the seat. "Motherfucker! Get down, Terri!"

The shots were coming in rapid succession. I heard the dull thud of bullets slapping into the car. I knew that it was just a matter of time before we were out of commission, either full of holes or the victim of a lucky shot to a tire.

The rear-window glass splintered in a shower of tiny shards. I shot Tommy a glance. He wasn't hit. I didn't think I was, either.

I vaulted into the back, hitting the rear seat face first.

Tommy glanced back over his shoulder for a nanosecond. Sweat was pouring down his face despite our newly acquired ventilation.

"What the hell're you doing?" he asked.

I ignored him. More rounds struck the car, one

lodging in the dashboard. I reached under
seat and pulled out the carbine.

Tommy caught my act in the mirror. "Ol

I balanced myself on the seat, extending the gun
out the shattered back window. Both cars were
careening all over the road. The chase had been
going on for about three minutes, but it seemed like
an eternity.

I pulled the trigger. Nothing happened.

"How do you shoot this fucking thing?"

Tommy turned briefly. "Jack one into the chamber!" I didn't know what he was talking about.

"The fucking handle on the right side, pull it
back! There's a selector switch under it, make sure
it's pointed down."

I pulled back the handle. I saw a round-headed
bullet slide into the chamber. I checked the switch,
a little protrusion, which was in the up position. I
clicked it down.

"Good girl," he said. "You're in business."

When I moved the selector switch to the down
position, I'd placed the rifle in full auto mode. I now
had a machine gun in my hands. Who knew? I
aimed the gun in the general direction of the Chevy
and pulled the trigger once.

The recoil held my finger back. Within two seconds, I unloaded the entire magazine, a banana clip
that held thirty rounds. The windshield of the Chevy
fragmented, and the driver's hands flew to his head.
The car swerved off the road into a wood line.

"I think I hit the driver," I screeched, although he
could have been struck by flying glass.

Tommy slowed down and craned his head to see.
The road was clear behind us. The only reminder
that a car ever pursued us was a lingering cloud of
road dust hanging in the air like a shroud.

He said, "Un-fucking-believable" and resumed his driving, this time at a sane rate of speed.

❀　❀　❀

About two miles down the road we passed a state trooper in a marked car. The cop did a double take when we drove by him. My new Eldorado looked like it had been in the first-wave landing at Omaha Beach. The cop tossed his coffee out the window, gunned his cruiser, and pulled us over.

The uniformed trooper approached the car with his gun drawn.

"What the hell happened here?"

Tommy was trembling, fear etched on his face.

"Deer hunters," I said, grinning like a fool. Tiny shards of glass were imbedded in my hair.

Within ten minutes, we had a three-car escort to the state police barracks.

❀　❀　❀

Tommy, despite a few well-placed kicks to his shin under the table in the interrogation room, told the cops the truth. He named names, said we were the targets of a vendetta by "the wiseguys in New York." He was scared; the hell with *omerta*, the Mafia code of silence.

My one phone call was to my uncle, who responded to the barracks within the hour.

Uncle Mike was a formidable figure. At just a little under six feet and weighing about 300 pounds, he demanded attention. He got it from the state cops. After my uncle spoke to them in private, we were told we could leave. The pending automatic weapons charge disappeared. Uncle Mike was a persuasive talker.

We told him the story. He locked us in a barn on another patch of family property about five miles from Wild Acres. He was back in a few hours with another car.

"Now listen to what I'm gonna tell you." He shot Tommy a dirty look.

"You take this fucking car and find a place to stay. Don't go back to the Island until I can make a few calls and say it's okay to go back home. We gotta assume it was the Bilottis. I gotta smooth this thing out."

❋ ❋ ❋

We locked ourselves in a motel room in Queens. No one knew where we were except Uncle Mike. He called after a few days, and I knew what he was going to say.

"Tell Tommy he's gotta return the dough. He don't return it, I can't be responsible. Joey also says that it wasn't them tried to kill you."

I never expected the Bilottis to admit they tried to kill Tommy. After all, I was in the car, and they could just as easily have hit me. My family wouldn't have liked that. Joey also said that they only wanted to talk to us that night in the diner parking lot. Sure.

"And if Ernst gets any ideas about takin' off," Uncle Mike continued, "make sure you don't go with him. Dickhead'll be able to hide until he decides to take off another brewery, and then they'll come and get him. He ain't gonna change, Terri. He'll bring you down with him. Tell him good."

Tommy had no intention of returning the thirty-five grand. To his way of thinking, a clean con where you got away with someone else's money was the same as working for it.

His plan, if you could call it that, was to wait a week, then sneak back to the house on Staten

Island, get everything we could jam into a car, and head for Florida.

"Couple of years," he said, "we come back, everything'll be forgotten."

❊ ❊ ❊

A week later, we snuck back to the house in the dead of night. It was warm for the first week in April, and I was looking forward to scooping up my belongings and heading south. I'd originally tried to talk Tommy out of what I considered a foolish move—I wanted him to pay back the money—but he was adamant, and I was in love. I looked at this as a chance at a new beginning.

So there we were, sneaking back into our own home like a couple of burglars. First we reconnoitered the block. Everything seemed normal. The few cars that were parked on the street were empty. There were no pedestrians in sight. Typical for a residential Staten Island neighborhood.

Tommy pulled the car two doors down from the house.

I was out of the car and halfway up the walk when Tommy popped the trunk and started after me.

Bushes rustled to my right. A man in a ski mask was crouched behind them.

I wailed my familiar refrain.

"Run, Tommy!"

I hustled for the front door as a bullet zinged over my head and crashed into the side of the house. I turned to see the figure, all in black, stand up behind the shrubs, fully exposed, a pistol in his hand.

Tommy skidded to a halt, momentarily undecided whether to run toward me or turn and race down the block. He turned and took off in the direction of the car.

The gunman raised a semiautomatic pistol and shot my Tommy four times. He fell as soon as he was hit, crashing face first onto the pavement.

I remember screaming. I remember lights coming on in houses, sirens, people trying to pull me off Tommy.

The ride to Richmond Hospital and the wait in the emergency room was a blur. I heard bells and someone calling "Code 99" over a loudspeaker.

The next thing I knew, I was surrounded by my family and a priest. A doctor came out of the operating room, his scrubs splattered with blood. He said, "I'm sorry."

I was thirty-three years old, and I felt like my life was over.

At the time, I was certain that the Bilotti brothers were behind Tommy's execution, but I was to find out later that all things are not what they seem.

1
The Family

My great-grandmother was a bookie. As the matriarch of the Debrizzi-Dalessio clan, she was the person who began it all.

Marie Debrizzi was born in Italy and came to this country in 1895. She settled in East Harlem, then a thriving, close-knit Italian community. Her husband, who died soon after they arrived, faded into the oblivion of family history.

Marie had one son, Alex, and two daughters, Teresa and Jenny.

She was way ahead of her time, a regular women's libber, believing that she could do anything a man could do and most times a helluva lot better.

Marie opened a candy store on 114th Street and Pleasant Avenue that had one large jar of stale penny candy in the window. That was the extent of her involvement in the confection trade. She ran a full-scale bookmaking operation from the store for years. She couldn't write in any language (she signed her name with an X), but could balance columns of numbers in her head, a feat that would make Meyer Lansky proud. By herself, she booked numbers, horse bets, and in later years, became a bootlegger. All without a man to front for her.

The infamous Dutch Schultz, the undisputed boss of the New York mob, was a friend of hers. He admired Marie for her business sense and balls. (She had to have a set stashed somewhere–hers was a tough business.)

She occasionally had hassles with deadbeat customers, gangs that wanted to muscle her, or the occasional stickup artist. The stickup guys had to be brain damaged. Holding up a mob-sanctioned bookmaker was akin to sticking your head into the muzzle of a fuse-burning cannon. Years later, some idiot burglarized a well-known Italian restaurant on the next block. They're still finding the fool's body parts. Even today, you can walk away from a Maserati with the engine running anywhere on Pleasant Avenue between 114th and 116th streets and come back to find it in the same spot. Probably freshly washed and waxed.

So whenever Marie had a problem, she could turn to Dutch, and he'd make it go away, immediately, if not sooner.

The only headache that wouldn't go away was her son, Alex. He was constantly getting into trouble. If he wasn't beating someone up just for the hell of it, he was burglarizing non-Italian businesses. He was generally a wild kid.

Dutch Schultz was often called upon to bail Alex out of a jam. Finally, the Dutchman had had it with the kid's forays into petty crime.

"Hey, Marie," he said one day during one of his many trips uptown to extricate Alex from his latest problem, "I think it's time you should get Alex to someplace he won't get into so much trouble."

Marie, I'm sure, probably frowned over the top of her glasses. "Oh yeah, like where?"

"Like Staten Island. It's like the country, almost. Trees, cows, all that shit. Oops, I'm sorry," the most feared gangster in New York said. My great-grandmother wouldn't allow bad language to be spoken in her presence and was known to dress down anyone who swore.

"Staten Island? You've gotta be kidding, Arthur. My business, it's here. I'm not going nowhere."

Marie Debrizzi was supposedly the only person in New York who could call the Dutchman by his given name (his real last name was Flegenheimer—she couldn't pronounce it).

"I'll give you the Island," Dutch told her. "You can control all the numbers, horses, everything."

"When should I leave?"

Marie Debrizzi was no dope.

And the empire was born. It was March 1924.

❋ ❋ ❋

Marie and Alex settled in the sparsely populated community of Concord, located on the eastern side of Staten Island, and promptly opened up a gin mill on Dekalb and Britton avenues. She called it the Webb Inn, choosing the name because the bar was made from trees whose grain resembled a spider's web. She was the bartender, cook, waitress, and dishwasher. She and Alex lived over the store in a large apartment where she also conducted her bookmaking business.

Within a short time, she bought the two adjoining buildings and expanded the Webb. Eventually, one of the buildings would become the headquarters for Dee's Cigarette and Vending Machine Company, but I'm getting ahead of myself.

Every day you could see Marie in her uniform: a housedress, rolled-down nylons, and black leather shoes. She wore her hair in a bun, as did most Italian widows. No matter how much money she made, she never indulged in fine clothes or jewelry. She was all business, but found more than enough time to keep her eye on Alex to make sure he stayed out of trouble.

Alex was very respectful of his mother, but he yearned to be a gangster. He made sure he didn't get caught doing anything illegal, knowing that Dutch Schultz would have been highly pissed if he had to journey to Staten Island to bail him out.

Alex married at twenty-three and had two daughters. He also had a girlfriend off Staten Island who bore him four children. He divided his time between the two families, and if either woman knew of the other, they kept their mouths shut. Alex also maintained his bedroom in his mother's house, using it to get away once in a while and eat some of momma's home cooking. Italian men, at least in those days, never strayed too far from their mothers.

Alex was a tough guy. He didn't take crap from anyone and never lost his fondness for fighting. He demanded, and got, respect. When he became head of the International Longshoreman's Association, he told everyone that ILA stood for I Love Alex.

I remember when I was a teenager, Uncle Alex would think nothing of punching out any of my boyfriends who disrespected me or the family or those he didn't like. When he got older, he'd send two of his goons to administer the beatings. I had a hard time holding on to boyfriends.

For all his crudity, he was good to his family (both of them). When his sister, Teresa (my grandmother,) lost her husband Dominic Dalessio, a dock worker, to an accidental fall into a ship's cargo hold, Alex took three of their children, John (my father), Alec (later called Pope, for reasons that are unclear seeing as how he wasn't particularly religious), and Mike (Mickey) under his wing. The remaining three, Giovanni (called Jumbo for obvious reasons), Mary, and Patrick, remained with their mother, who never remarried. Italian widows in those days mourned their dead husbands until it was someone's turn to mourn *them*.

By this time, Alex had a minicriminal empire. His mother was getting old, and she turned over the daily operation of the family business to him. With youthful vigor, he expanded the bookmaking business to include loan-sharking and sports betting.

It was into this atmosphere that his sister's boys matured and became part of the Debrizzi empire. Jumbo, Patrick, and Mary stayed legitimate, probably due to the fact that Alex didn't raise them. Patrick was killed during the Anzio landing in World War II, and Mary was to spend her later years in a mental institution, where she remains today. Jumbo was in the vending business until the day he retired, never turning a dishonest dollar in his life.

The Dalessio name morphed into the diminutive Dee, because non-Italians often confused Dalessio with Debrizzi.

As they entered their twenties, the boys became active in Alex's gambling business. He instructed his nephews well. My father once told me that Alex gave them advice that they never forgot.

"I'm the one person feared by many. You guys are three and should all be individually feared. In numbers, there is strength. Don't ever forget that money and power buys it all. Push your weight around, bust heads, pop 'em, let their bodies wash up on the beach. Don't ever take no bullshit from anybody. An eye for an eye; a tooth for a tooth. But remember, hurt them only when you have to. You can't be a cowboy, or you'll learn the hard way." The gospel according to Alex.

Wire rooms were set up all over Staten Island. Men sat around taking bets at all hours of the day and night. One of the biggest rooms was located next to my Grandmother Teresa's house. Phone lines were strung from the main house to a small house in the backyard. I remember that my father had unused phone lines installed in the main house to fool the cops into thinking that we were taking action there. Those lines were constantly tapped, while the real phone equipment was never touched.

As the business became more diverse, my father's natural leadership qualities surfaced. Alex couldn't be everywhere, and my father took more of an active role in helping him run the various rackets.

My father was a natural mediator. While Mike had a fiery temper and would break a gambler's legs if he was in arrears, my father would sit down with the deadbeat and work out a payment arrangement. Pope had the same temperament as Mike, so my father was always smoothing out arguments and other business problems.

"Don't cowboy it," he'd tell his brothers. "There's the right way, the wrong way, and the Dees' way."

The Dee brothers, now realizing profuse wealth, bought lavish homes that could be construed as mansions. My father's house was on Emerson Hill, part of a wealthy, established Staten Island neighborhood. My father took advantage of the elevation by installing a still in the middle of the living room with ventilation pipes running through the ceiling. "This is beautiful," my father said. "The smoke just blows out over the Island, you can't smell the friggin' fumes."

The brothers also went into legitimate businesses with their ill-gotten gains. Over the years, they owned Dee's Cigarette Vending, several Studebaker automobile dealerships, real estate, Dale Lumber Company in Pennsylvania, and a Dumont TV dealership. My younger brother, Patrick, appeared on the cover of the first *TV World* magazine because of the family's affiliation with Dumont.

By the 1930s, Pope, Mike, and my father had married. They all dressed in handmade suits, Italian leather shoes, and diamond pinky rings. Most everything they owned was monogrammed, including the toilet paper. All drove obligatory black Cadillacs.

My father met my mother at a club on Staten Island. For Ruth Crocker and my dad, it was love at first sight. My mother's mother however, wasn't enamored of my father because the Dee brothers' reputation was widespread on Staten Island. There wasn't a warm body on the Island, other than raccoons, that didn't know that the Dee family controlled gambling and shylocking. My mother's father was a policeman killed in the line of duty while investigating a burglary in Chinatown before my father came into the picture.

My mother was a beauty. At five-seven, with a stunning figure, she was modeling for the prestigious Powers Agency when she met my father. She had the most striking green eyes you could imagine, and while a natural brunette, she dyed her hair red all her life. They made an impressive couple, with my father an imposing and handsome man. He was about her height, with dark Italian good looks. He loved the good life, including the best food and wine, and early into his forties, he had put on considerable weight. But he was always elegantly dressed, manicured, and polished. The Jackie Gleason type. Theirs was a love story that withstood forty years of the turmoil that is inherent to an organized crime family.

❋ ❋ ❋

My father proposed to my mother from jail.

Even though the Dees were paying off the police, they had to take an occasional bust to make it appear that the local vice cops were doing their job. It just so happened that it was my father's turn to do a few months when he decided to pop the question. From his cell, he wrote her an eloquent and touching letter asking for her hand in marriage.

The day he got out, July 18, 1936, they were married in a lavish (what other kind?) ceremony. They both wanted children immediately. My father, naturally, wanted a boy to carry on the Dee name. My mother didn't care, embracing the familiar tune that she only wanted the child to be healthy.

I came along on July 17, 1937, very much a girl. My dad, however, was to make sure I was tough like a boy. The first time he held me, my mother would often relate, he called me Tiger, and he continued to refer to me by that sobriquet until the day he died.

2

Little Tiger, Child of Privilege

The night I was born, my parents were in the Latin Quarter, Manhattan's premier nightclub, owned by Lou Walters, Barbara Walters's father. The club was a mecca for top echelon mobsters, politicians who would have a tough time explaining how they were able to afford the prices, and major movie and Broadway stars.

My parents got the royal treatment from Walters; the best table, finest wine, best service. Nothing was too good for John Dee, then at the pinnacle of his power as one of New York's top mob bosses, a peak he would stay perched upon for another forty years.

My father and mother loved the night life, loved the party, the attention. If they weren't at the Latin Quarter, they were fixtures at Mamma Kelly's or Lindy's. My mother always made certain that a fully packed suitcase was in the trunk of the Caddy whenever they went out, which was almost every night, certain that when the time came to have me, she'd be out clubbing.

Her premonition came true. As she told it, she

and my father had just settled into a stage-side booth, anticipating the show, which she told me was headlined by either Jimmy Durante or LaVerne Baker, two entertainers she apparently got confused after imbibing a few cocktails, a habit she picked up soon after her marriage.

Above the din of preshow conversation, my mother said to my father, "John, I think my water broke."

My father, who was distracted because he was working the room with waves and smiles to the powerful and subservient, said, "Yeah, yeah, I'll get a waiter."

"No, *my water broke*. It's time."

My father turned to face her. "Time? What time? We've got fifteen minutes yet," he said, referring to the kickoff time for the show.

I think my father was in denial. The last thing he needed was having my entrance into the world witnessed by a roomful of drunks, or worse yet, making the newspapers the next day. In those days, mobsters tried their damndest to keep a low profile, a direct contrast to today where wiseguys vie for cover stories in *People* magazine.

Years later my father told me that he hustled my mother out of there right past gossip columnist Walter Winchell's table, who smiled and asked him what was new.

"Same old shit, Walter. Gotta go."

They arrived at New York Hospital in the nick of time.

❋　❋　❋

I was "Tiger" from the day I was born. My father preferred the nickname to Theresa, and whatever my father wanted, he got. Fortunately for him, my mother didn't object.

32

I was pampered and doted upon, especially by my father. He would give me money or presents on the sly so my mother wouldn't know. She caught him a few times slipping me a bill or a brightly wrapped gift, and she would say, "You're going to spoil her, John," and made him promise not to do it again. As soon as she turned her back, I'd get another present. While the first words most children are able to understand are "mommy" and "daddy," my first words were strung together to form the sentence, "Don't tell your mother."

My first memories were of affluence. While other families struggled to obtain gasoline because it was needed for the war effort, the Dees were floating in the stuff. My family had a steady supply of stolen ration books. Others walked, we drove. Everywhere.

I was a pretty kid, having the elegance, refined beauty and grace of my mother more than the dark good looks of my father. I was treated like a debutante as soon as I could walk. If there was a lesson to be had, a skill to be learned, I had the private tutors to teach me.

Ice-skating lessons came first. Twice a week, my mother and I would journey to either Madison Square Garden—the one on Eighth Avenue and Fiftieth Street—or the Rockefeller Center skating rink for my private lessons. My mother sought out the custom skate maker who crafted Olympic champion Sonja Henie's ice skates and had him make me a duplicate set to the ones she wore when she copped her first gold medal. I remember other kids doing pirouettes on skates with cloth uppers. Mine were suede.

I became quite good, and once my mother thought I'd mastered the ice, she got me into horseback riding. The first order of business was to buy me a horse. This was where my father came in. He knew from horses since he ran the largest book-making operation on Staten Island, if not the entire city. The horse was boarded and pampered at Clove Lake Stables on the island. That horse saw more TLC than the British royal family. My father made sure the stable people were tipped generously, and they couldn't do enough for little Tiger.

❋ ❋ ❋

I went to a private grammar school, and while most of the kids had well-heeled families, no one came close to having the money and power of the Dees. Of course, I was too young to know that my family's entitlement came primarily from gambling, so I sailed through my younger years blissfully unaware.

While the closest my friends ever got to the New York Yankees was listening to them play ball on the radio, I had the team at my house on numerous occasions for dinner. Over the years, almost every player enjoyed a Dee Italian extravaganza. I was a princess, and royalty isn't into baseball, so I didn't know a New York Yankee from the guy who deliv-ered our milk, but the boys in school were impressed. When I was in my late teens, however, I remember Mickey Mantle being at our house one Christmas. Everyone knew the Mick, even me.

Over the years the house was a magnet for celebrities. Boxer Rocky Marciano and my father liked to put away bottles of guinea red late into the night. My father had a picture of him and Vic Damone taken in the den that he liked to tell people was shot before Vic had gotten his new nose. Louis Prima and Keely Smith were also there a lot. Keely was the only female ever allowed to go hunting on the Pennsylvania estate. She knew her guns, and I was jealous. From as early as I can remember, I had an affinity for guns and begged my father to teach me how to shoot.

"You're a girl, Tiger," he'd say, "girls aren't supposed to play with guns."

"But Keely's a girl," I'd protest.

"She's a big girl."

End of discussion.

❋ ❋ ❋

My family's lifestyle first affected me when I was seven. My father had been in and out of jail over the years for his periodic gambling busts, but I was too young to know what was going on. When I was in the second grade, he figured that I'd get wise to the reason for his occasional absences, so he and my mother concocted what they thought was a perfect plan to keep me and my six-year-old brother in the dark. They enrolled us in boarding school for the duration of my father's eight-month prison stretch.

The St. Johns Villa Academy on Staten Island was run by a bunch of nuns who made Hitler seem like Shirley Temple. I was used to getting anything I wanted, but the nuns had a different way of handling things. Corporal punishment was the order of the day, and I could count on a smack or a paddle on the ass almost daily. My brother, John, and I hated it and were convinced, as only children can be, that our parents didn't love us anymore and had cast us aside.

I proceeded to make life for the nuns a living hell. My brother was a year younger than me, a frail kid, and stayed on the sidelines while I wreaked havoc, the object being expulsion and a quick trip back home.

"We're gonna go home if they have to carry me out of here on a stretcher," I told my brother.

I went to work.

The first order of business was to harass my candy-ass schoolmates, who were about as rebellious as a nun in a coma. I'd wait until they were asleep, then toss them out of their beds. They ran straight to the mother superior. I'd pitch fits during mealtimes, throwing food and cursing like a sailor. I also began to eat toothpaste, thinking that the nuns would assume I was nuts and expel me. All I got out of that was the sweetest breath and sorest ass in school. After three weeks of this, I was physically worn out, with only a black-and-blue backside to show for my efforts. Clearly, my master plan wasn't working.

One day I was blissfully chewing gum, a felony as far as the nuns were concerned, when the mother superior asked me what I was doing, thinking that I was going to lie to her whereupon she could give me a good ass-kicking with God's blessing.

"I'm chewing gum," I said, much to her astonishment.

She looked like a penguin on steroids. She was huge, mean, and only smiled when she was paddling me.

"Well, then remove it, young lady, and report to my office," she said. I knew what was in my future.

"Sure, you old bag," I said, smiling, and promptly spit the wad of gum in her face.

I couldn't sit comfortably for a week, but the next day, John and I were back home. Enough, apparently, had been enough.

Fast-forward thirty years to when my cousins attempted to enroll their kids in St. Johns Villa Academy. They were refused admission because they were Dalessios. My name still reverberates in those hallowed halls. At seven years old, I had become a goddamn legend.

✳ ✳ ✳

I continued my wild ways, still convinced that my parents didn't love me. While at St. Johns, my mother never came to see us on weekends, the only time relatives were permitted on school grounds. My aunt came every Saturday, however, and I'd jump around like an excited puppy when I'd see her shiny black Caddy cruise up the school's circular driveway. My mother, I later discovered, was in the beginning throes of an alcohol dependency that would plague her health in later years; she spent most weekends hung over.

I developed a fondness for fighting. I didn't care whether you were a boy, girl, ten years older than me, or a sumo wrestler. If I went into one of my rages, watch out. My parents put me on the 1940s version of tranquilizers for a while, but they didn't work. They made me wilder, more out of control. So they gave me the ultimate tranquilizer: Grandma.

My father's mother was the linchpin of the family. In most Italian families of the era, the grandmother was the ruling matriarch, consulted on matters of importance and respected for her years. My grandma was a kick-ass disciplinarian. She never hit me, mind you, but her stare was enough to turn my spine into jelly. I called it the stink eye, and it could bore holes through cement.

I was even a match for grandma, however, and it took all her energy to keep me under control. She'd confine me to the front yard outside the house; I wasn't permitted to stray from her sight. She'd be in the kitchen, cooking as usual, with a good view of me through a window. She had one eye on her sauce, the stink eye on me.

I promised to stay in front of the house. You'd sooner lie to the pope than to grandma. I didn't want the wrath of the stink eye, so I stayed put.

I did, however, throw rocks at everyone who walked by. As word got out that a seven-year-old psycho with an aim like Annie Oakley was pelting anything that moved with rocks the size of potatoes, the neighbors steered a wide path around Grandma Dalessios's house. Of course, every now and then, a stranger would amble down the block, and I'd baptize him with a boulder. I once brained an air raid warden who knocked on grandma's door one night to tell us that a blackout was in effect and we had to turn off the kitchen lights. There was a war on, after all, he said. I elected to turn off *his* lights and leave the kitchen lights on. Mission accomplished. I was a fun kid.

Grandma took a lot of flak from the neighbors and began to try to confine me inside the house. I rebelled, stink eye or not, and she would have to drag me inside. After a while, this wore her out, so she came up with the phone-call ploy.

"Terri!" she'd holler from the kitchen. "You got a phone call!"

As soon as I was inside, she would lock the front door. I was under house arrest. The phone-call trick worked more than you would imagine. I guess it doesn't take much to fool a seven-year-old, no matter how sharp I thought I was.

❋ ❋ ❋

Eventually, I calmed down. My parents figured the more love and attention they showered on me, the more I'd be a good kid. For the most part, they were right.

As I hit the double digits, I was still in the dark about my family's involvement with organized crime. My father's jail stints were described to me and my brother as "business trips," and we believed the lie. The carload of FBI agents camped out in front of our house on an almost-daily basis taking pictures of everyone who came and went were described to us as private security guards employed by my father because we were rich and "gangsters might want to harm us."

When I turned twelve, I began helping my father run his weekly card games. These weren't the floating games that my father ran around Staten Island, which attracted hard-core professional gamblers. Those games were constantly moved to avoid raids by cops and the occasional ripoff artists who insanely thought that holding up a mob-sanctioned game was an easy score. The games that I attended took place in my father's den and were frequented by his closest friends.

I thought that every father had friends called Broadway Joe, Duke, Paddy the Priest, Nick the Pope, Numnuts, and Meathead. My favorite nickname belonged to a skinny guy everyone called Couldn't Shoot Straight, for reasons I never discerned.

The den was every man's dream. The walls were covered in rich leather, and there was a fully stocked mahogany bar in one corner. The card table was custom made with shelves on the underside for each player to rest drinks, food, and cigars.

My job was to empty the ashtrays and get new cards from the wall safe. These games were marathons, often lasting eighteen hours. Eventually, the cards would get tacky and worn. Little Tiger to the rescue. My father made me wear white linen gloves, so in the unlikely event of a police raid, my fingerprints wouldn't be on the safe or the wall next to it. He told me that the gloves were necessary to keep the cards clean, and of course, I believed him.

I got my first taste of real money at those games. The players were more than generous. Every time I emptied an ashtray or got someone another sausage sandwich, I'd get a five- or ten-dollar bill. At the end of a game, I'd have $300, big money in 1948. I'd turn all the cash over to my mother, who would put it in the bank for me.

Around this time, I began accompanying my father on his "collections." Once a week, we'd cruise the Island in the Caddy and make stops at people's houses so my father could collect debts owed from various gambling operations. The money was given to him by men who ran games around Staten Island, not individual gamblers who incurred losses. This was, in fact, my father's weekly tribute, a right for a mob boss. Either the Dees sanctioned your game, or you didn't have it.

Of course I was completely oblivious of the real reason for the trips. He'd just say, "C'mon, Tiger, let's make the rounds." I'd stay in the car (usually parked illegally), so we wouldn't get a summons, while my father scooted into someone's house. He'd emerge seconds later carrying an envelope or paper bag.

I loved those times alone with him because it was rare that we had much time together. Between jail time, infrequent as that might have been, constant meetings with underlings, and he and my mother going out every night, I didn't get much personal time with him.

❊　❊　❊

My parents were pleased that I had calmed down. They had one less thing to worry about. But my brief flirtation with passivity came to a crashing halt when I was fourteen.

A boy in school began to tease me, saying that my father was a gangster and my entire family a bunch of hoodlums. I lost it and proceeded to beat the crap out of him. This episode garnered me a brief suspension and denials from my father when I confronted him about the accusations.

"We're businessmen, Tiger, we make lots of money. Some people are jealous. Don't pay them any attention."

A few days later, a newspaper article was left on my desk at school detailing my family's involvement in organized crime. The article was long and specific, showing how my father's criminal empire had grown over the years. It also mentioned how many times he had been arrested and the length of his jail sentences.

I was crushed. I cried for days, locking myself in my room and skipping school. Weeks later, when I finally came out of my depression, I began a journey down a self-destructive path that would control the rest of my life.

3 The Rebel

I viewed my family's lies as a betrayal of my trust. I may have been only barely into my teens, but the newspaper article coupled with my exile to St. Johns Villa Academy put me over the edge.

I turned my depression into anger and began acting out. The target of my wrath was my parents–I wanted to punish them for lying to me.

I decided to steal my mother's car. When I entered my teens, the Dee family deserted their Cadillacs en masse and switched to Chryslers, the reason remaining forever lost in our family lore. It undoubtedly had something to do with a profit incentive; most Dee family decisions were motivated by how much money could be made.

My mother, by this time, was a certified alcoholic. A Scotch drinker by design, she'd often switch to vodka martinis to break up the monotony. However, she left the house sober every morning for a marathon-shopping spree in Manhattan. She rarely missed a day in Saks, Gimbel's, and the pricey stores on Madison Avenue.

I was intimately acquainted with my mother's

daily routine. She would drive her new black Chrysler to the ferry terminal (this being before the Verazzano Bridge was even a thought), park in the lot, and sail off to "the city."

My girlfriend, Tina, and I would skip school and be minutes behind her on a bus. With the extra set of keys I had made up from a neighborhood locksmith, Tina and I would steal the car, tour the Island in grand style, and have the car back in the lot, often in a different space, before my mother came back laden with packages on the four o'clock ferry.

It made little difference where we parked the car because by the time my mother got off the ferry, she was loaded. She would have at least seven drinks in her and always assumed that she had forgotten where she had left it. Sometimes it would take her a half-hour to find the car. Once, she couldn't find it at all, but that story comes later.

This went on for months, maybe twice a week. I drove all the time, never getting a peep of protest out of Tina. It was always assumed that I would drive; hell, it was my mother's car.

One day Tina decided that it was her turn behind the wheel.

"But you never drove a car before," I argued.

"I've been watching you. It seems pretty easy."

We debated for a while, finally deciding that Tina would drive in a deserted area of the Island where there were no people and better yet, very few cops. She floored the behemoth eight cylinder for a ride that had us careening out of control until we were abruptly stopped by a tree.

In the 1950s, Chryslers were the sturdiest things next to tanks, nary a piece of plastic in them, but they were no match for a deep-rooted elm. The tree demolished the front end and took away my will to live. I was certain that my father would kill me.

Our plan was to distance ourselves as far from the wreck as possible, but we were picked up by cops in a patrol car about a mile from the accident scene. They asked us if we had anything to do with the car wrapped around the tree down the road.

"Not us, officer," I said sweetly. "We're on our way to our grandmother's house." It worked for Little Red Riding Hood, why not us?

"You with her?" one of the cops asked Tina.

Tina folded like an old dollar bill. "I didn't mean to do it, officer. It was an accident, I swear." My friend Tina obviously wasn't raised in a mob family where you would sooner cut your throat than give yourself up.

We were taken to the local precinct, and when the cops found out who my father was, they called him through his answering service. He showed up alone, seething.

He stuck his finger in my face. "I'll deal with you later," he said and vanished into the detective squad room. Tina was shaking like a tin sign in a hurricane.

"Your dad's gonna have us killed," she wailed.

"Shut up, Tina."

They had us on grand larceny auto, a charge I knew my mother wouldn't press, and driving without a license, which could have us in court to pay a fine. My father didn't need the notoriety, and when he emerged from the squad room minutes later, I knew he had bought our freedom.

"Out," he growled.

He didn't say a word to us for the entire ride home. Once there, he called Tina's parents, explained what happened, and asked if it was okay for him to punish their daughter along with me. They acquiesced (no one objected to whatever John Dee asked), and he put us to work scrubbing the kitchen floor on our hands and knees, a modest punishment to be sure. Deep down I knew he wouldn't hit me. He'd threatened many times over the years to whip me with a belt, but never laid a hand on me.

Neither he nor my mother said a word about the incident afterward. To this day, I think he was somewhat proud that I'd pull a stunt like that. It was something a boy would do.

❋　❋　❋

My father wanted to keep a tighter rein on me so he began taking me to the various bars where he had his jukeboxes. The jukebox business was controlled by several organized crime families, and my father liked to visit the bars that did business with him, checking to see that his equipment wasn't being vandalized and to show the owners that he was a hands-on boss.

He had the same routine all the time. We'd go into a bar, my father would wave to the bartender, order a club soda, drop a fifty-dollar bill on the bar, and walk out. I realize now that the tactic created goodwill and that it was good for business.

My father had his hands full, both with me and my mother. By this time, she was drinking all day, and I was a temper tantrum away from becoming a sniper. I recall one time my father was going to Chicago to meet with Sam "The Plumber" DeCavalcante, the boss of the Chicago mob. My father, rather than leave my mother home alone, decided to take her with him.

They were scheduled to fly to Chicago late one afternoon, the time of day a favor to my mother who didn't want to miss a day of shopping. As flight time neared and my mother was nowhere to be found, my father left without her. Later he found out that my mother had gotten so drunk in Manhattan that she had forgotten where she had parked her car on Staten Island and couldn't find it after staggering around in a circle for an hour.

I was no angel, either. My father couldn't watch me all the time. I began hanging around with an older crowd and drinking. If it was good enough for my mother, it was good enough for me. I was fourteen, but looked eighteen, and very popular. I wasn't interested in boys so much as boyfriends as just friends. I was basically one of the guys.

One day I had two friends, Ralph and Pete, over to the house when we should have been in school. Because the friends happened to be males, it caused me to run away from home when my father thought he saw something that he really didn't see. A classic case of bad timing.

Ralph was about to enter the bathroom and was loosening his belt. My father chose to walk into the house at that moment and saw Ralph with his belt flapping in the breeze. He automatically assumed that I'd just had sex with both boys and proceeded to bellow like a moose. He called me things that made me cry and rage at the same time. I was still a virgin, but didn't plan to stick around and try to explain my chastity to my infuriated father. I took off right behind the two boys, and we didn't stop moving until we hit Pennsylvania.

We hitchhiked all the way to the Poconos, where my grandmother was now ensconced at Wild Acres, the family estate. I may have given her a hell of a time in the past, but I loved my grandmother dearly and knew that she would be the only one that could talk some sense into my father.

After two days on the road, sleeping under trees with very little to eat, looking like refugees, we finally came within striking distance of grandma. Still, we were too exhausted to go on, and when we spotted a vacant farmhouse, we decided to break in and get some sleep, not to mention a decent meal. Up until that time, we'd subsisted on milk and juice that we'd stolen from front porches.

We got in through an open window, and I raided the refrigerator, making a fourteen-year-old's version of a gourmet meal. I cooked anything that wasn't frozen. We ate like kings, after which we took turns in the shower, then put our same grungy clothes back on.

We stayed the night, not giving a damn whether the people who owned the home returned or not. The next morning, I was the first one up and was poking around a closet when I came upon three rifles and several thousand rounds of ammunition in tin boxes.

Ralph and Pete decided to go hunting. While they were gone with two of the rifles, I decided to shoot up the house with the third. It was a spur of the moment decision, my rage pent up and simmering. By the time I was through, the place looked like it had weathered a frontal assault from a Ranger battalion.

In the meantime, Pete and Ralph were picked up by the cops as they walked along the road with loaded rifles. They gave me up immediately, and six police cars jammed with troopers screeched to a halt in front of the house while I was outside blasting the windows.

"Drop the friggin' gun!" a trooper screamed. All I saw were the barrels of six revolvers. I dropped the gun. I had been wearing my hair jammed under a leather motorcycle hat, jeans, and a shirt that was too big for me. One of the troopers threw me on the ground and slapped me hard on the head before cuffing me, causing my hat to fly off and sending my hair cascading around my shoulders. The troopers were shocked to see that I was a girl.

Three hours later, my father showed up at the state police barracks to iron things out. The damage to the house was later estimated to be $7,500, which he paid, and our freedom cost him another $1,500 in bribe money. My father had a subdued talk with Ralph and Pete out of my earshot before we got into the car to go home. I tried to talk to them in the car during the drive, but they wouldn't even look at me. My father had scared them speechless.

Back at home, I expected the worst. I knew I wasn't going to be beaten, but I expected another trip to a boarding school or worse. Instead my father sat me down and hugged me.

"Hey, Tiger, I just want to say that I'm sorry I said the things I said the other day. I know who you are and that you wouldn't do those things with those boys. I jumped to a conclusion."

I felt vindicated and a little cocky. "You made me run—"

He held up a finger. "Did I make you shoot up that house? You know how much money it cost me to get you out of that jam?"

I shuddered and stammered for a while trying to come up with something clever. He shook his head. "I don't know what I'm gonna do with you." Then he got up and left the room. I was a good girl for the next few weeks, a personal record for me. Then I wound up putting twenty-five live salamanders into my grandmother's piano just for the hell of it. I had gathered them in one marathon session in the woods behind her house. When she sat down to play, the little lizards started bouncing out of the piano. I thought it was a riot, but I guess you had to be there.

As for Pete and Ralph, they avoided me for about a month, then we resumed our friendship, but keeping a low profile, or so we thought.

One day I was supposed to skip school with them to raise a little hell. They didn't show up at the designated time and place, so I hunted up a girlfriend, and we spent the day avoiding the cops. I later found out that word had filtered back to my Uncle Mike that Pete and Ralph were back in the picture, so he had them beaten up. After they recovered, they wouldn't even walk down the same side of the street with me.

※ ※ ※

I was a habitual truant, and the school could do nothing to get me to attend. My father, however, had his own private army of truancy officers. He had the local police on the payroll for years and put out the word that any cop who spotted me out of school would get $50 to grab me and call him. It got to be a regular thing. At least twice a week, he'd get a call to come retrieve me from the local precinct station house. A lot of those cops paid their mortgages with the bounty money.

I grudgingly went to school after that because my freedom would always be short lived. Capturing me on the street during school hours was more alluring to the cops than bagging Willie Sutton, the bank robber, who was public enemy number one at the time. At least grabbing me would put food on the table. Locking up Willie would get a cop a medal. Can't eat a medal.

I finally threw in the towel and quit school. My father didn't object because all the bribes he had given to the cops weren't doing me any good. As soon as they deposited me back in the classroom, I'd take off again. My mother, by that time, was drunk most of the time and didn't really care what I did, just as long as I kept her out of it.

The only reason I'd attend on the days that I did was because I was either too worn out from the previous day's partying or I had no one to play hooky with. I'd wind up falling asleep in class, and the teachers would tell the other kids to let me sleep because it was the only way I could stay out of trouble.

❋ ❋ ❋

My love of guns almost proved my undoing. I liked to go to the deserted side of the Island and practice target shooting with a rifle I'd bought on the street for twenty bucks.

I had a favorite spot down by the ocean and was soon joined by my girlfriend, Grace, who had similar interests. We built a lean-to we called the Fort and popped away at targets for hours. When we got tired of that, we would swing on a tire suspended over the water. Simple pleasures for simple kids.

One day, two boys I knew from school tagged along. While Grace and I were gathering wood to make a fire, one of the boys decided that it would be a cool idea to balance the rifle, barrel down, on his foot.

"Hey, jerkoff!" I hollered, "The thing could go off. Take the rifle off your foot."

"I checked," he said. "It ain't loaded."

Know-it-alls tended to piss me off (of course, it was all right when I thought *I* knew everything), so I walked over to the kid and said, "You sure about that?"

"Of course I'm friggin' sure. Whaddaya think, I'm some kinda asshole?"

I reached down and pulled the trigger. The responding blast was muffled by his shoe as the round passed through his foot and lodged in the dirt. He let out a scream that could be heard in New Jersey.

I had proven my point. Now it was time for the cover-up. While the kid squirmed on the ground holding his wounded hoof, I gave orders.

"Grace, bury the rifle. You," I said to the last man standing, "go out on the road and flag down a car, we gotta take Gimpy here to the hospital."

The only vehicle on the road was a garbage truck. We got the driver to take us to a local hospital where the attending physician called the police, as he was obligated to do whenever he treated a gunshot wound. If I would have known that, I would have left the kid to limp home, because I knew that if the cops came, my father would not be far behind. It wound up costing my father $1,000 to bribe the cops to keep me out of jail, plus he paid the kid's medical bills. I was grounded for a month.

❋ ❋ ❋

When I turned eighteen, I begged my parents for a car.

"Don't you think you should get a license first?" my father asked.

"Never needed one before."

"Well, you're gonna get one now."

I practiced driving for months, only to fail the road test three times. To me, a red light was a suggestion. On my fourth try, my father once again bailed me out. He bribed the examiner.

"Think she'll pass today?" my father asked, as he

slipped a palmed hundred dollar bill into the examiner's hand.

"Don't see why not," he replied, then took the next applicant.

I never even got behind the wheel. The license arrived in the mail the following week. I was beginning to understand that I could get away with anything due to my father's influence, a dangerous realization for a kid with my temperament. I was untouchable, and I knew it.

Until I reached eighteen I was a hell-raiser, a problem my parents anguished over at the time, but days they would look at as fond memories compared to the problems I gave them when I discovered sex.

4 Sex and the Single Wise Girl

I blossomed when I was sixteen. I had always been a pretty girl, but now I was causing car wrecks. Once when I was crossing Victory Boulevard, a guy behind the wheel plowed into the car in front of him while craning his neck to check me out.

At five-six and 135 pounds, I was built like the proverbial brick shithouse. Long, bleached blonde hair cascaded around a face that sported high cheekbones and pouty, bee-stung lips. I had a huge chest, tapered down to a wasp waist, with shapely legs honed from years of ice skating and horseback riding. Teenage boys in the neighborhood, hormones raging, voted my ass top honors in their Best Ass Contest, a dubious distinction, but ego inflating to a nubile teenager.

I became what two of my father's business associates thought was an easy target. One afternoon I was walking along Hyland Boulevard, a busy commercial area, when I heard a horn honking and my name being shouted.

"Hey, Terri, over here!"

A neighborhood wiseguy, whom I knew as Bebe,

about twenty-five and a gofer for my father, was beckoning me to his car, a new Chevy. He offered me a ride home. Naively, I accepted.

After we passed the turnoff for my house, I smelled a rat.

"You're going the wrong way, Bebe."

"It's okay, I just wanna show you something." Bebe was always squiring around a local girl. He was tall and not as good looking as he thought he was, and at the time, I considered a twenty-five-year-old guy ancient. Besides, he worked for my father, and even if I liked him, I wouldn't go there.

Bebe wound up showing me a deserted lot near the beach, miles from my home. After he lunged for me and we wrestled for a few minutes, I figured he'd eventually rape me unless I uttered the magic words.

"Let me go, or I'm going to tell my father."

He dropped me like I'd just grown a penis. After that, he drove me home like the nice little asshole that he was. He must have asked me fifty times if I was going to tell my father about what happened.

"I'll think about it."

I never said anything to my father, but I'm sure the next few weeks saw Bebe's balls shrunk to the size of BBs.

A similar incident occurred with another of my father's friends. Cincy, about thirty, fat and as alluring as a wet sock, saw me running my palomino, Shawnee, at the stable, and I guess he let his little head override his big head.

It was a hot summer day. Fully clothed, I rode Shawnee into Brady's Pond, about three miles from my house. I'd done this often on sultry, humid days. The horse loved it, and it cooled me off, too. Unbeknownst to me, Cincy followed me in his car and watched from the shoreline. When I got out of the water, he was leering at me like I was a winning lottery ticket.

"Why don't you tie the horse to the door handle and sit by me for a while?" he suggested.

"Why don't you tie your dick in a knot?" I countered.

Warped as Cincy was, he thought this to be a come-on because he laughed, grabbed me, and pulled me off the horse and directly into his convertible.

I wasn't about to waste my time tussling with the creep, he'd probably get off, so I just repeated the refrain about telling my father. He let go of me like I was a porcupine. He apologized profusely and later became vice-president under Bebe in the No-Balls Club, both of them acting like eunuchs whenever I was around.

I had similar problems with other older men, but still I was a virgin. Then I met Tommy Ernst and that became a thing of the past. It was love at first sight, a true love/hate relationship that went from moments of unbelievable tenderness to passionate fights.

I met him at Ronnie's Snack Bar, located on the beach in Staten Island, a hangout for teenagers. Four years older than me, he worked as a melter for Bethlehem Steel, but moonlighted as a thief. When we first met, he had just stripped his current girlfriend's house of all its copper plumbing while she and her parents were out of town. He sold the metal to my Uncle Mike at a cut price, but still made good money on the deal.

We hit it off immediately and consummated our relationship a few months later in the backseat of his car. We went together for three years, all of it on the sly. At that time, most any boy I dated would be shown the door by my father because they weren't up to his standards. If they persisted in trying to see me, my Uncle Mike would have one of his goons beat them up. My family knew about Tommy's criminal inclinations, so he definitely wouldn't pass Dee muster. Even years later, when we renewed our relationship after my two divorces, and Tommy built us a gorgeous house, and my father saw that I was happy, it took over a year for him to warm up to him.

Like any relationship, the warts didn't come to the surface until after we knew each other for a while. Tommy was very controlling; he had to know where I was at all times. I would often spot him parked in front of my house, waiting to see if I got home late and who got me there.

We had numerous arguments until finally I couldn't take it anymore. One day at Ronnie's Snack Bar, I read him the riot act.

"Tommy, we're through."

"What do you mean, through? You mean for like today? You want me to take you home?"

"No, listen carefully." It was like trying to teach a kid to tie his shoes. "I don't want to see you anymore. We're done, through."

"So you want to leave now? I'll get the car."

That was it; I exploded. I took a plastic bottle full of ketchup and squirted him with it. He looked down at his shirt, wiped some ketchup from his face, and said, "You'll rethink this tomorrow, Terri. I'll get the car."

The second salvo was with mustard. He was very colorful. This time it was his turn to get pissed off. He screamed and lunged for me. I took off with him in hot pursuit.

I was pretty fast, but no match for his

endurance. Tommy was gaining on me, and I saw my salvation in a phone booth, the kind with the accordion door that has since gone the way of the dinosaur. My plan was to jump into the booth, slam the door, and jam it closed with my leg. The best laid plans....

I got into the booth okay, but when I shut the door, Tommy kicked at it with such force and speed that I couldn't stop it with my leg. I stopped it with my face instead. Result: a broken nose.

There was blood everywhere; I looked like I had taken a direct hit in the face with a mortar round. Tommy, realizing what he had done, or worse yet, whom he had done it to, became very apologetic. He rushed me to the hospital, where he paced the floor like an expectant father, awaiting word from a doctor as to the extent of my injuries.

Fortunately for Tommy, my Uncle Mike showed up at the hospital because my father was out of town. Normally, Uncle Mike was the muscle in the family, my father the negotiator. Had my father been around, however, I'm sure the roles would have been reversed.

After Uncle Mike ascertained to his satisfaction that I wasn't in a life-threatening situation and would recover, he sat a trembling Tommy down in the emergency room.

"Listen, kid, this is what's gonna happen. You listening?"

Tommy nodded like a woodpecker.

"You're gonna go away for a while. Don't be bothering my niece again, you got it?"

Nod, nod.

"I tell you why I'm doing this and not burying you," Uncle Mike said. "You wanna know why?"

"Uh huh."

"Because you're a good earner. You made us money with the copper thing. This I don't forget, so you got a ride. This once only. Bye now." And at that, he got up and turned his back on Tommy, my boyfriend's signal to get out of Dodge.

Tommy and I wouldn't get back together again for ten years, but not for his lack of trying.

❋ ❋ ❋

I told my father that I had broken my nose when I took a tumble off my horse. I don't know whether he believed me or not, but he didn't give me the third degree.

I began dating a young man named Frank Aron. Frank's father was a bookie and ran one of my father's wire rooms. This made Frank acceptable as a date. He was soft spoken and seemingly kind, a facade that would make a hasty exit later in our relationship. At the time, I took him at face value, and he treated me well. But I wasn't all that serious about Frank, and I made it plain to him that I was still eligible.

Shortly thereafter, I met Louie Grasso. Everyone called him Chickie. He was twenty years old and quite good looking. Within weeks, I was smitten. Within months, I was pregnant. While Chickie promised to stand by me and seemed genuinely happy with my condition, this was a big problem, not only because in the 1950s it was a scandal if an unwed girl got knocked up, but because my father was John Dee, and if he found out, Chickie would get plucked and skinned.

The good news was that my father was away at the time for his periodic trip to "college" as he called it. There was no hiding his jail time now, not since I'd read about it in a newspaper article, but he couldn't bring himself to use the word "prison" in my presence. He had eight months to go to complete his "semester" when I'd entered my third month. I decided to keep everyone in the dark except my girlfriend, Margo, who accompanied me to my doctor's appointments and lent me a shoulder to cry on. I knew, deep in my heart, that I'd have to give the baby up for adoption, realizing that my father might go off the deep end if he found out and have Chickie killed. He might be sorry afterward, but the deed would have already been done. My doctor, a family friend who was sworn to secrecy, said he would arrange for space in a home for unwed mothers in Manhattan.

I began to show in my fifth month and needed an excuse to get out of the house until I had the baby. I made certain that my mother was good and soused before I sprang my bullshit story on her.

"Mom, I got a job in Miami, I'll be gone for about five months."

"Be sure and write, dear," she said and took another sip of her martini.

"Don't you want to know what I'll be doing?" I wasted too much time coming up with a plausible story to let it go untold.

"Okay."

I told her I was selling real estate. I even gave her the address and phone number of a friend in Hallendale in case she got curious. If she called, my friend would reach out to me, and I'd return the call from Manhattan. No caller ID back then.

While I was crushed at the prospect of having to give up my baby, I still had Chickie. He had given me an engagement ring, and at least we had each other. We were planning our future when I became the victim of what I was later to call The Great Blow Job Conspiracy.

When Tommy Ernst heard that I was engaged to Chickie, he began a campaign to win me back. He felt that enough time had passed, and he now had the right to reenter my life. He knew nothing about my pregnancy. Whenever he called me, I would hang up on him, but he caught me one day in my grandma's house. The phone rang, I picked it up.

Before I realized that it was Tommy, he blurted out, "What if I told you that Chickie and his friend, Dave, are in a car right now with two girls, and they're going at it hot and heavy?"

For once in my life, I was speechless.

"Well? Terri? You there?"

"I don't believe you."

For the next ten minutes, he did his best to persuade me that he had just driven past a deserted spot by the beach, notorious as a lover's lane, and he'd seen Chickie and his friend steaming up the windows with two girls. He begged me to go there with him so he could show me that Chickie was cheating. After a while, I relented.

"Okay, I'll go, but no funny stuff." He swore he'd be a prince.

I met Tommy on a street corner a few blocks from my house. After I got into the front seat of his car, he told me that as we approached the car Chickie and the girls were in, I was to duck down so I wouldn't alert him. Tommy would tell me when to look up.

As we got near the beach, Tommy said, "Okay, get down now. I'll tap you when you should get up."

I ducked down and awaited the signal. About a minute later, I got the tap. "Now."

I shot up, expecting to see Chickie, his friend, and two girls. What I saw was Chickie and his friend, Dave, alone, standing by the car drinking beer. They were staring directly into Tommy's car when my head bobbed up, giving them the impression that I was giving Tommy a blowjob.

Chickie's jaw dropped. Tommy yelled, "Man, she's good," and drove away.

Tommy, I later found out, had sent his buddies all over the Island to find Chickie. Then he set up The Great Blow Job Conspiracy.

I was in tears.

"I did it for your own good," Tommy said. "Chickie's an asshole."

"I'm pregnant, you stupid piece of shit. We're engaged!"

Before he had a chance to react, I jumped out of the car at a red light and ran home as like I was on fire. Chickie was waiting for me in his car. He was livid. He started out by calling me a whore. From there it got worse.

"Chickie, it was a setup, I swear," I cried.

"Bullshit. What were you doing, bobbing for apples?"

You've got to understand the times and the Italian macho thing to understand Chickie's reaction. Within an hour, it would be all over the neighborhood that his fiancé may or may not have given some other guy a blowjob. He was honor bound to make a federal case out of it.

As far as I was concerned, if he didn't believe me, I didn't want him for a husband. I threw my engagement ring in his face.

"Keep your fucking ring, we're through," I screamed and stormed into the house. I never saw him again.

❋ ❋ ❋

I left home for "Miami" in September, just as I entered my sixth month. I had gained thirty pounds, but my mother was oblivious. She started drinking right after breakfast, and by noon I could have looked like Kate Smith and she wouldn't have noticed.

The home was located on the Upper East Side and run by nuns, my favorite people. My doctor sent me money every week, bless his heart. My one extravagance was coloring my hair, which was strictly forbidden by the nuns. The others preggos would act as lookouts so I could sneak into the bathroom and dye my hair. Other than committing that one violation, I stayed in my private room and cried until it was time for me to deliver my child.

A few days before I went into labor, my doctor examined me and told me that I would have to have a Cesarean section.

"Wonderful," I said, "go for it."

"Not so wonderful. This is surgery. Your mother's going to have to sign for you."

Great.

I put off notifying my mother until two days later when I went into labor. Now I had no choice but to call her.

"Mom, it's Terri."

"Soooo, how's Miami, dear?" She was loaded. It was eight o'clock in the morning.

"I'm not in Miami, Mom, I'm in Manhattan."

"Manhattan, Florida?"

Oh, Christ. "No, Mom, New York." I gave her the address, then I told her I was about to give birth and needed her to sign off on the C-section.

It took a while for the information to sink in. "Okay, this'll work out. I'm due at Saks for a fitting at noon. I can stop by right after that. That okay?"

"Yeah, Mom, wonderful."

"Anything you need?"

Yeah, a new mother. "No, just write the address down." I repeated it. I kept my fingers crossed that she wouldn't wind up on a plane bound for Florida.

✳ ✳ ✳

The home had its own delivery room. As I was being wheeled in, my mother showed up, drunker than I'd ever seen her. She was carrying her lunch, a corned beef sandwich and a chocolate malted, and was dressed like she was going to tea with Mamie Eisenhower.

"Hello, honey. You okay?" she slurred.

By that time, I was in so much pain I would have let them rip the kid from me with a soup ladle. "Yeah, just great. Sign the goddamn paper, okay?"

She was guided to a seat by a nurse. It took my mother a good minute to prepare herself to sign the paper. She cleared her throat, examined the paper closely without really seeing it, turned it over, adjusted her glasses numerous times, and picked imaginary lint from the page. A regular Ed Norton.

"Jesus, Ma, sign the goddamn thing, will you!" The pain was excruciating.

"Sure, honey." And she scribbled her name.

"Okay, doc, start cutting!" I bellowed. My mother stayed in the room for the delivery, all the time chowing down on the sandwich and slurping the malted. To this day, I can't stand the smell of corned beef.

On December 23, 1955, Karen Ruth Grasso made her entrance into the world. Her father was nowhere to be found. Shortly after the birth, my mother took off for places unknown, probably to the 21 Club for a bracer.

They let me hold my daughter for a few minutes before trying to take her away from me. I screamed worse than when I was giving birth, refusing to let go of the baby. It took three nurses and a hypo loaded with enough drugs to subdue King Kong to make me relinquish my daughter. It was, and remains, the saddest day of my life. I would not be reunited with her for forty years. My father would not find out that I'd had the baby for thirty-nine.

While I was in the home recovering, Frank Aron, the guy I'd dated casually, came to see me. He was very solicitous and loving.

"Listen, kid, anything you need, you ask, okay?"

I was touched.

While Chickie never showed, his father did. He felt it was the right thing for him to pay for my hospital bills and boarding. I didn't argue nor did I ask about his son.

A few weeks after I got home, my father "graduated" and returned to the family. I was still sore from the surgery and had to sit down and climb stairs carefully. He was home two days when he noticed that I was walking around like an old lady.

"You okay?"

"Yeah, just a little sore."

"From?"

"The horse. Got thrown."

"First a broken nose, now this? You gotta get rid of that horse."

❧ ❧ ❧

Frank Aron became a frequent visitor. Before long, we were an item, my father approving because of Frank's father's affiliation to my family.

On October 6, 1956, we were married in an elaborate ceremony (what else?) At Tavern on the Green, a catering hall on Staten Island.

I became pregnant within a year, which kept my

new husband out of the army. My son, Lenny, was born in 1958, followed by my twin boys, Ronnie and Frank, in 1959.

The abuse began almost immediately after the birth of the twins. Frank, for no apparent reason, developed a jealous streak.

He accused me of having sex with everyone from the mailman to our parish priest. I barely had time to have sex with *him*. I had three wailing babies to take care of. But there was no reasoning with him.

Frank became cruel almost beyond description. He began picking fights, which escalated into physical abuse. I was burned with cigarettes and hot spoons and beaten with wooden clothes hangers. In late 1959, I spent a night in the hospital due to one of Frank's thrashings. Fortunately, he was tender and loving with the kids.

Through all this physical abuse, I never went to my father for help. He genuinely liked Frank, who kept his violent side very much a secret. I had disappointed my father for years with my behavior, and now I didn't have the heart to burst his bubble when he thought that I was finally happy and leading a normal life.

Frank's father, I came to find out, beat his mother on a regular basis. Very few people know about that, either. It didn't take Columbo to figure out where my husband learned his behavior.

I finally got up the nerve to take my babies and leave Frank, telling my father that we'd had a simple failure to communicate and that I needed time alone. It was a classic midnight move. While my husband was out, I split. Within a short time, however, he found out where I was and came looking for blood.

I thought I was safely ensconced in my new

apartment in a two-family house on the other side of the Island when the door splintered open one afternoon while I was in the kitchen. Frank had broken in and was in a foul mood.

"Leave me, you fucking cunt? You'll leave me in a fucking box!"

By the time he reached the kitchen, I was out the window, dressed in a half-slip and bra. This was the exact moment my father had chosen to pay me a visit. He was pulling into the driveway behind Frank's car when I came bursting out of the alley, half-naked like a bit player in a Russ Meyer soft-porn movie.

I ran directly into his arms. The jig was up. Within minutes, he knew the real story behind my breakup. Luckily for Frank, a neighbor had spotted me screaming in my underwear and called the police, who arrived minutes later, sirens blaring. Had my father been able to get his hands on Frank, my husband would have been one with a car crusher at a local junkyard.

I needed a break. I took my children to Florida for an extended stay. In September 1960, I divorced Frank.

I was a single mother with three toddlers and had no intention of sponging off my family. I had gotten myself into this mess, and I was going to survive by my wits.

5 Marrying Into the Mob

I stayed in the Miami area with a girlfriend who helped me take care of the babies. Frank had no idea where I was. My father sent money as needed, and while I didn't want for anything, I was getting bored. Knowing that my ex-husband was still in New York kept me from going back, however. Given his jealousy and propensity toward violence, I knew I was better off being bored than dead.

Then some good news. I was in Florida about a year when my girlfriend, Margo, called and told me that Frank had remarried. Good for me, but I felt sorry for his new wife.

I returned to Staten Island and rented a two-bedroom apartment in a two-family house located about twenty minutes from my parents. The place was bright and cheery, although a little cramped.

First on my list of things to do was to find a nanny to watch my kids so I could go to work. I was determined not to sponge off my parents. My mother would stop by about once a week on her way to the ferry and yet another shopping binge and throw money at me. I would have liked it better if she spent some time with the kids, but that wasn't her thing. Self-indulgence, that was her thing. My father came around whenever he could, but with an ever-expanding operation, we saw less and less of each other. Of late he was also going legitimate, opening a vending and cigarette distribution business that would one day become one of the largest on the East Coast, a company I would run.

There was also a young guy who worked in the grocery store down the block who had a definite Terri jones. A few weeks after I moved in, I found a small bag of groceries resting against my door. I thought that perhaps my father had brought them by and left them when he discovered that I wasn't at home. I checked with my father, but he claimed that he didn't leave the groceries. Then it happened again, only this time it was a larger bag. This went on for a few weeks. Finally I asked my neighbor—the street yenta, every block has one—to watch the house and report back to me if she saw anyone dropping off bags of food while I wasn't home, then I took the kids to my parents' house for the afternoon. Sure enough, when I got home, I had another bag of food on my doorstep.

My neighbor told me that the stock clerk from the grocery store dropped off the bag of food as soon as I left the house. The neighbor pointed him out to me when he was sweeping the sidewalk in front of the store. I never even knew the guy existed though I'd shopped in his store from day one.

At first I was going to tell him to stop the deliveries. I assumed that he was stealing the food and didn't want him to get caught, which would eventually happen. But then I thought better of it and even began smiling at him when I was in the mood for sirloin.

I never even considered asking Frank for child support or alimony because he would then be a part of my life forever or at least until my youngest, the twins, turned eighteen. I saw how Frank's father's brutality had made Frank a violent adult, and I didn't want my boys exposed to that kind of behavior, otherwise the cycle would likely continue.

After interviewing a dozen potential nannies, I chose an older German woman named Elaina. She was in her early sixties and had raised four boys of her own. Now widowed, she wanted to help raise someone else's sons. She turned out to be great. My kids loved her, and she was firm but fair with them.

Realizing that I'd always had a big mouth, I decided that a sales job would be right for me. I searched the want ads in the *Staten Island Advance* and immediately vetoed any inside positions. Bad enough I was confined to a small apartment, I didn't want to be counter-locked in some department store.

I took a job, believe it or not, selling Bibles door to door. The man I worked for, Nathan Edelman, was Jewish and distributed the Bibles citywide.

I showed up at his home on the Island, which doubled as an office, dressed for the part. Besides a black business suit with a properly long skirt, I wore opaque nylons and a ruffly white blouse. My hair was bunned up tight enough to ricochet bullets.

Edelman was about sixty, wore a yarmulke and thick glasses. He gave me the once-over.

"What are you, some kind of ex-nun?"

"Far from it, but I'm here to do God's work."

"Great, you're hired."

If I was Charlton Heston dressed up like Moses, I couldn't have sold more Bibles. I was a natural. The first thing I did was boost the price of a bible from $60 to $70, then let the mark (I mean customer) talk the price down to the original $60. Then I got a brilliant idea that would make Martha Stewart proud. I took trade-ins.

"But we've got a family Bible," the typical customer would say.

"Not like this," I'd say and whip out the book. It was impressive: leather bound with gilt edging, fully illustrated and weighing in at about five pounds. My Uncle Mike could have used them instead of cement shoes. I lugged around six of them. After three months, I had arms like Schwarzenegger.

"Well, I don't know...."

"Tell, you what," I'd say, "this Bible goes for seventy dollars. I'll give you ten dollars for the one you've got, no matter what kind of shape it's in."

Invariably, I'd get the sale.

And so it went. But after five months, tramping all over Staten Island began to lose its appeal. I talked it over with my friend, Margo.

Margo and I had been friends since grade school and remain close to this day. Unlike me, however, she came from a "normal" family. That didn't keep her from raising hell right along with me, though.

When I was going through my gun phase as a teenager, I'd balance an apple on Margo's head and shoot it off with a .22. One time, I accidentally backed over her with an old hand-cranked Ford coupe. Little wonder that Margo liked to drink.

"This Bible thing is a dead end," I said. "I need something different, something with a future."

"Let's go on a vacation."

I could always count on Margo to come up with a sensible solution to any problem.

We wound up at a resort in the Poconos, not too far from Wild Acres. I took the boys, and we played with them during the day at the pool. At night a babysitter watched them, and Margo and I went out partying. Margo was looking for a man. If a decent guy came along and swept me off my feet, I wouldn't object, but after Frank Aron, I wasn't really looking. Besides, I figured I was destined to remain single. It's a rare kind of man that will take on a new wife and three little boys.

Margo, however, had hope. Now in her midtwenties, quite pretty but still single, she was getting desperate; the times dictated it. During the early 1960s, if you weren't married straight out of high school, you were an old maid. She eventually married a successful banker, got pissed off at him one day and stabbed him. But that's another book.

We had been at the bar for about an hour goofing on the nerds trying to score with us when I spotted a good-looking guy staring at me. He was about my age with a movie star's chiseled face and broad shoulders. He also sported a little paunch. I wasn't perfect either; I could overlook the gut.

He ambled over, and we began to talk. Margo took a walk.

"Hi, I'm Tony Buttino."

I introduced myself as Terri Dee, the Dalessio name being well known in the area. I didn't want to raise a red flag with a possibly decent guy. My family's reputation was enough to cool down any man. Tony told me he was from the Lower East Side of Manhattan, owned a bar called the Dew Drop Inn and the grocery store next to it, and came to the Poconos occasionally to get away from the city. It turned out that the reason he came to the Poconos was true, but his mother owned the two businesses.

Tony worked full time at being a gambler, alcoholic, and momma's boy. Also, like every other guinea in the neighborhood, he flew pigeons, a hobby that always mystified me. You get to watch a bunch of birds fly around in a circle for twenty minutes, then you clean up bird shit for the rest of the day. Fascinating.

We began dating when I got back to New York, and it wasn't until several months into the relationship that I discovered his secrets. His mother, Jenny, supported him when his luck was running poorly, which was most of the time. She also doted on him; Tony could do no wrong. Whatever he needed, he got—money, clothes, cars. Even though he made a show of hanging around the bar like he contributed to its success, anyone could see that his mother ran the show. But he wasn't a loud or abusive drunk. Most of the time, you'd never know he went near a bottle, something that would change as our relationship deepened.

Quite a catch, huh?

I was at a stage where humping Bibles around in a suitcase and taking care of my boys was beginning to wear me down. Tony had five middle-aged aunts who took care of my kids almost better than I did. They were all widows and lived to pamper them. They were also very nice to me. I wanted security, and the Buttinos saw to it that the boys and I got everything we needed and then some.

Within six months, Tony moved me and the kids into an apartment above Volpe's Bar on Lafayette Street in Lower Manhattan. His aunts were fixtures in the apartment, catering to our every need. Tony's mother would stop by often and shower us with gifts. So while I had to put up with Tony's vices, the bennies were worth it, or at least I thought so at the time.

One thing that I liked about Tony's family was that they weren't "connected," or at least didn't seem to be. Naturally, everyone in the neighborhood knew wiseguys. This was Little Italy, not Scarsdale, and mobbed-up people used to come in and out of the bar all the time.

I was sick of my family and the Dalessio infamy. I wanted a normal life or at least as normal as I could get. By this time, Tony knew all about my family and its history, warts and all, but he didn't care. He definitely wasn't involved with the mob, with his drinking and gambling, they wouldn't have wanted him even if he volunteered. Tony was satisfied with hanging out at his mother's bar all day and pretending to be a big shot.

About six months into the relationship, Tony asked me to marry him. I knew I was going to say yes, even though I couldn't say that I was in love with him. I was, however, in love with the lifestyle. He was good to me, though, and I had some feelings for him. Right after he proposed, I sat him down and told him I would marry him, but I wanted reassurance that my family wasn't a sore spot with him

"Why should that be important?" he asked.

"My family, particularly my uncles, have a hard time accepting the men in my life."

"Hey, to know me is to love me."

"You don't care about the family business?"

Tony looked perplexed. "Why should I? You know who my sister lives with?"

Tony had only one sibling, a sister named Olympia. Olympia was a bit mysterious, for reasons I was about to find out. She lived in the neighborhood with her husband and three kids, I was told, but didn't come around much. Whenever she did visit, it was always with the kids, never hubby.

"Her husband, no?"

Tony smiled and stroked his chin.

※　※　※

Vincent "The Chin" Gigante was a well-known mobster, even back then. Today he's the head of the Genovese crime family, but at the time, he was an underboss, having gotten his bones, rumor had it, by blowing away Murder Incorporated boss Albert Anastasia while he was enjoying a shave in the Park Central Hotel in 1957.

Tony told me in a hushed voice that his sister was Chin's piece on the side. Tony called it a common-law marriage. They'd been seeing each other for years, and he was the father of the three kids.

Great. The Dalessios were part of the Genovese crime family and had worked with Chin for years. He and my father were good friends; I'd heard the name mentioned in subdued tones many times. There I was trying to get away from the lifestyle, and I was being sucked back in, like Al Pacino in that last awful *Godfather* movie.

These days, at seventy-five and now the boss of the family, Chin is residing in a federal penitentiary doing a twelve-year bit, a sentence the feds fought for for fifteen years. The Chin, it seemed, had a unique defense, never before used by a Mafia boss. He claimed mental illness, or at least his lawyers did. He was supposedly too infirm to aid in his own defense. He would be rolled into court every day in a wheelchair, wrapped in the same ratty old bathrobe.

In 1985, when Chin was trying to persuade the courts that he was crazy, I came up with an idea, albeit a little tongue in cheek, which I called the Bimbo Defense.

Chin was married to a woman named Olympia, and they had three kids. His mistress, Tony's sister, was also named Olympia, and *they* had three kids.

"Hey, Dad," I said one day after too many glasses of Chianti, "why don't Chin's lawyers say he's gotta be demented because he purposely chose a bimbo with the same name as his wife and had the same number of kids so he wouldn't get confused?"

"Very funny."

The Chin could be seen wandering around the Village near his Sullivan Street clubhouse, supported on either side by two beefy guys, while wearing his signature bathrobe, drooling, and talking to himself.

This act worked for many years, and he kept a tight rein on his criminal empire. No one was allowed to mention his name. Doing so was an automatic death sentence. If you referred to the boss, you stroked your chin (a rather difficult sound to pick up on an FBI audio tape). Even today, in the middle of his sentence, he still controls the family, although he has dropped the psycho act. He walks a mile every day; a miracle, proclaim his lawyers. As this book is being written, Gigante has been indicted for perjury (the mental-case act) and for continuing to allegedly run the family through his son, Andrew.

"So how come I've never met him," I asked Tony.

"He likes to keep a low profile. We get married, you will."

Tony assured me again that his family was legitimate, that they had nothing to do with the mob. I still believed him, and we decided to get married, but I would soon find myself in a sit-down with Chin on a matter of family values.

❋　❋　❋

The marriage ceremony and reception were attended by more than four hundred Buttinos, Dalessios, and friends. Chin was there, too, along with a convoy of federal agents parked outside the church, snapping pictures like we were royalty. The day went smoothly, both clans partying heartily.

I became pregnant almost immediately. The Buttinos were overjoyed. I was also thrilled. My mother said, "That's nice, dear." My father was enthusiastic. Everything looked rosy, and I delivered my son, John, in July 1962. It was a rough birth, and I knew immediately that there was a problem when they whisked him away from me.

After fourteen hours, I was frantic. What had they done with my son? Finally my doctor came in and broke the news, the baby had died shortly after being born. Dr. Knapp, who had delivered all my children, explained that he had considered me too sick to take the news right away. I had had a life-threatening delivery and was listed in serious condition.

To say that I was devastated would be an understatement. I went into a deep depression. If it wasn't for the Buttinos, I wouldn't have survived. They took care of me while I was bedridden for four months suffering from a complete nervous breakdown and complications of the delivery. My mother and father took the boys while I was on the mend. I wasn't hospitalized because my in-laws insisted on taking care of me, but if they didn't watch me constantly, I was apt to do something destructive.

One day, one of the aunts turned her back, and I began cutting up the linoleum floor in the kitchen with scissors for reasons that I couldn't explain. It just seemed like a good idea at the time. When I wasn't destructive to inanimate objects, I was destructive to myself, often pulling hair from my head. It took months before I was back to my old self and was able to resume taking care of my boys.

※　※　※

Almost immediately, I became pregnant again, this time delivering a healthy eight-and-a-half-pound boy, whom we also named John, on July 23, 1963. As soon as my son was born, however, things began to change.

The Buttinos, who had been overly solicitous since I'd met them, were now ignoring my kids and me and lavishing all their attention on the new baby. He was a Buttino, you see, and my other children and I weren't.

We were all but completely ignored while baby John was treated like the Christ child. There was always an aunt in attendance to moon over the boy. *I* even had a hard time getting near him.

During holidays, the baby would be showered with gifts while my other three boys were given hardly anything. At the baby's first Easter, Chin stopped by with $500 for the baby and $250 to be divided among my three boys. In addition, the baby wasn't permitted to sleep on the same sheets as my other three sons, his had to be laundered and ironed every day. After a year of this treatment, I'd had enough.

I told Tony that we were moving. At first he whined and complained, saying that he didn't want to be separated from *his* businesses, but of course the real reason was because he couldn't bear to be away from his mommy.

Finally, after months of arguing, and with the blessing of his mother (we had to have that), we moved to Staten Island. The one proviso in getting permission from Jenny was that we let her buy us our first home. At that point, I was willing to live in a tree house just to get away from the Buttinos, so I agreed. I, however, picked the location.

We moved into a beautiful home right around the corner from my parents. Because of the distance from Manhattan, we saw less of the Buttinos, which meant that they were at our house three times a week instead of seven.

※　※　※

Tony began to change. He started to drink more and became abusive. He never hit me, but he threatened a lot. He knew that if he laid a hand on me, I'd deck him, so words were his weapon of choice. Tony, in addition to all his other failings, was a bit of a pussy. I'd raise my voice, and he'd run.

One of the reasons I married Tony was to become independent and put some distance between myself and my family. So here it was, a few years later, and I was living practically right next door to my parents. It's like the bird with one short wing and one long wing. Every time it tries to get somewhere, it continues to fly in smaller concentric circles until it eventually flies up its own ass. I just couldn't get away from my family. And now I was beginning to wonder if that was really a bad thing.

Things came to a head with Tony at a party at the home of one of my father's most influential (and legitimate) business associates. The party was held poolside. Both he and his wife were in their early sixties and were very well bred and elegant, a pleasure to be around. Tony, who was invited along with the rest of my family, was late.

He finally arrived when we were about three hours into the party. He was drunker than I'd ever seen him, so shit faced that he could hardly walk. He staggered to the bar by the pool without so much as a "hello" to my parents or our hosts. My father pulled me aside.

"Get this asshole out of here, or I'm going to have to do it myself." He was steamed.

Before I had a chance to get to Tony, he had wandered over to our hosts, slurred an introduction, and promptly tossed both of them into the pool, fully clothed. He thought this was a riot and actually peed in his pants because he was laughing so hard. I was mortified.

My father dragged Tony off the grounds by his hair. I was angry and frustrated; angry for the shame he'd brought on my father and frustrated because I felt helpless to change Tony. Out of blind rage, I did the first thing that came to mind.

I grabbed a steak knife and slashed the tires on his car.

He was sitting on the curb nursing a red bruise over his left eye, courtesy of my father, when I dropped the knife in his lap.

�֎   �֎   ✖

After the pool incident, our relationship took a nosedive. Tony was drinking even more, and he began to see other women. He tried to be subtle about it, but one day when he staggered into the house with his fly undone and lipstick on his underwear, I got the message.

I'd lay into him verbally, and he'd threaten me with a beating. Tony, being the wuss he was, talked a good beating, but couldn't walk the walk. One day, however, he came home drunk as usual and saw a bruise on little John's knee. He went berserk.

"You're an unfit mother," he yelled, followed by a stream of curses.

I had no idea what he was talking about. "What?"

"John's leg. What the hell happened to it?"

The bruise was the size of a dime, you had to strain to see it. "Kids, Tony, they run into things. No big deal, calm down."

"If my mother ever saw that, she'd explode. She'd take the kid."

That did it. I got right up in his face. "You're mother ever tries to take my son, I'll wipe the streets up with her."

Tony balled his fist and wound up. "You fucking cu—"

I decked him with a hard right to his nose. His eyes bulged, and he grabbed his face, coming away with a handful of blood.

"My nose! My nose!"

I kicked him in the groin. "Now it's your balls, your balls!" I screamed.

He doubled over, rolled on his side, jumped up, and ran out of the house. He was still gone three hours later when I got a phone call from my father. He sighed loudly before he said hello.

"Now you're beating up your husband?"

I told him what happened. "He deserved it. How'd you find out, anyway?"

"Tony ran to his mother; his mother called her daughter, Olympia, who told Chin, who called me. Terri, I don't need this shit. Tony's an asshole. You can't work it out, divorce him."

Tony came home the next day, sober for once. I was civil. We agreed to try harder in our marriage, Tony assuring me that he would quit drinking. Sure.

Three days later, he was at it again, drinking heavily. This time he waved a steak knife at me in the kitchen. I wrestled it from his hand and proceeded to beat the crap out of him. I pummeled his face repeatedly, while he covered up and cried. Toward the end of the melee, he attempted to run from the house. After initially blocking his path, I let him go. I wasn't proud of myself. I cried, not so much for what I'd done to my husband, but for my poor track record in picking men.

I woke up the next day to an empty bed. As I swung my legs to the floor, the phone rang.

"Hello," I said, expecting it to be Tony.

"It's Vincent. We gotta talk."

❋ ❋ ❋

I met Chin outside of his clubhouse on Sullivan Street. This was the 1960s, and he wouldn't start his crazy act for another few years, therefore he was alone and dressed decently. I was scared witless. After all, I had been using his bimbo's brother for a punching bag, an *Italian* man no less.

"Let's walk," he said and hooked my arm.

Chin originated the "walk and talk," often attributed to John Gotti. Chin thought it was much harder for the feds to record a conversation while he was moving. Back in those days, he was right. These days, the FBI could record the Roadrunner hitting mach one.

I didn't know whether I was going to be threatened, killed, or given a beating. It turned out to be none of the above.

"Tony's a fucking idiot," he said as we rounded Bleeker Street. "I know about the drinking, the broads, the whole bit."

"You're not mad at me?" I said, already decompressing.

"Mad? Let me tell you something about your asshole husband. He's into one of my bookies for five

83

large. I told this bookie that once the money's paid, he's to take no more action from Tony. He takes the action, I told him, don't expect to be paid. He's a thorn in my fucking side is what he is."

"So why are we talking?"

"I want you to do me a personal favor and let the jerk alone. I don't want any phone calls from my wife about how you beat the shit out of Tony. She calls me, I gotta call your dad. This I don't want to do. *Capesh?* Try to work it out. You can't get a friggin' divorce."

❈   ❈   ❈

I gave it one last shot. Within three months, I had gone into business for myself. I distributed women's human hair wigs citywide with ten women working for me. The business was based out of my house, and I was making good money. An extra-added benefit was that I was always with my children.

Tony saw it differently. He insisted that my business was taking valuable time away from the kids, and he demanded that I give it up. I wasn't about to. I think it was more about Tony being a failure in life and me beginning to make something of myself that aggravated him.

Of course, he went for me again, with the usual results. Only this time, I faked a punch to his head, and he ran out of the house crying.

Three months later, we were divorced. I had my kids, but didn't want child support. I also didn't want to go to battle over the house. I signed over my share of our home to him. I told Tony that I wanted him out of my life, and he complied.

6 Crime 101

Free once again. This time I vowed to stay away from men for a while and concentrate on my wig business. In the first few months following Tony's departure I devoted all my time to the business. I moved into a spacious apartment on the other side of the Island and set up shop. I increased my sales staff from ten to fifteen women, each responsible for a section of the city. They sold wigs to hairdressers, boutiques, and even door to door. I had a few super saleswomen who could actually do that.

The money was rolling in, and I was happy, although a little overwhelmed. If you led the kind of life I was used to, it can be a bit difficult making the adjustment from being dependent on a bunch of old ladies, with little to do for myself, to paper shuffler, which was exactly what I was doing. I was elbow deep in sales orders, tax forms, and delivery schedules.

One afternoon I was returning home from the post office with a box full of someone else's hair when I decided to stop for a sandwich at a diner I'd never been to. Normally I wouldn't do this—I took my lunches at home while I made phone calls, and I usually wouldn't stop in a place I was unfamiliar with. But I was hungry, and it seemed like a good idea at the time.

It was late for a lunch crowd, about two o'clock, and there was only one other customer besides myself, a man sitting at the counter with his back toward me. As I passed him, heading for a window booth, I heard my name.

"Hey, Terri, you don't say hello?"

I turned. Tommy Ernst.

He was smiling ear to ear, those white teeth lighting up the whole room, contrasting a deep tan. In his early thirties now, he was a bit heavier–but he needed the weight. His hair was a bit shorter, dark, and slicked back. There was a pipe sticking out of a leather tobacco pouch on the counter. All this wrapped in an expensive charcoal-gray suit, crisp white shirt, and rep tie. He looked like a banker or stockbroker.

"Hi, Tommy." I felt weak in the knees. It had been thirteen years since we'd been together, and I realized that I still loved him.

He swung around, patted the stool next to him. "Sit."

I sat. We talked for what seemed like hours. He told me that he was the owner of Shertam, a Sheetrock and insulation business. He did work all over the Island. Within a year, he said, he'd be the biggest seller of gypsum on the East Coast.

"Give up your old ways?" I asked.

Tommy smiled. "Once a thief, always a thief, but you can't steal twenty-four hours a day, you know?"

We had lunch and the afternoon melted away. I forgot all about making phone calls, sending invoices, and everything else that just two hours ago I had considered urgent.

❋   ❋   ❋

We began dating. My friends used to tease me that I never dated, I just got married. This time I was determined to take it easy, hoping that the third time would be the charm. My father wasn't crazy about Tommy; he'd always been overly critical of the men in my life, but my Uncle Pope liked him. Tommy told me that he was selling all his swag to my Uncle Pope, who was realizing a nice profit. In my family's circle, Dracula would have been an insider as long as he bootlegged hot blood through them.

After six months, we moved in together. Neither of us had marriage on our minds, and we liked our arrangement the way it was. Tommy remained a gentleman and was particularly good with my boys. To them, he was daddy, and he relished the role.

I continued with the wig company, but I wasn't looking to build up the business. Tommy made a good-enough living for the both of us, and I liked the idea of having more time to spend with him and the boys.

As time passed, Tommy became more open with me about his extracurricular activities. I suppose he figured that after a year together, he knew he could trust me.

The Sheetrock and insulation business was doing well being run legitimately, but Tommy wasn't satisfied unless he could scam his customers. He had a virtual lock on the trade on Staten Island and decided that he could make three times as much money if he didn't actually install insulation, but charged as if he had. He would Sheetrock over hollow walls and tell his customers that he had installed insulation. Today there are thousands of homeowners on Staten Island who think that their homes are properly insulated and take out their frustrations over unseemingly high heating bills on the utility companies.

Once Tommy saw that he was getting away with this scam, he went one step further. He would contract to Sheetrock and insulate a multistory commercial building or dwelling and invoice for four workers on each floor, a logical number of men to do the job competently. In reality, he would have the same four guys do the work on the entire structure. He got away with this because by neglecting to install insulation, they were doing half the work and saving hours and material for which the customer would get billed. While customers were charged for union workers, Tommy used nonunion slave labor. He called these men googans, for a reason that he never shared with me. Within short order, Tommy was rolling in money.

He decided to build us a house. And what a home it was. Completed after a year, it had five bedrooms, a yard that seemed as big as a golf course, a three-car garage, and a wraparound deck, all constructed with stolen materials, nonunion workers, and hijacked machinery. He insisted on picking the neighborhood where our dream home was to be located, choosing one of the Island's more exclusive areas.

"You want to know why our house is gonna be here, Terri?"

"Gee, Tommy, maybe because it's better than living near the projects in Stapleton?"

"No, wise-ass." He got a faraway look in his eye. "When I was a kid, like five, seven years old, we lived right down the road here. We were close to the rich people, but just on the other side of the tracks. I tried to make friends with the other little kids around here. No one would talk to me because I was the poor kid. They'd throw crap at me, make my life miserable. Well, fuck 'em. Tommy Ernst has arrived."

I knew now that it all went back to his youth. The world, as he knew it, shit on him; now it was his turn. The hurt he had endured as a kid drove him to make more and more money, no matter how he had to earn it or whom he had to harm. He rationalized that he was some sort of contemporary Robin Hood (emphasis on the "Hood"), and he got a kick out of stealing from people with money.

Tommy would go to great lengths to make a score, often getting a legitimate job at a company he was going to rip off just to gather intelligence. He liked to target companies that produced, shipped, or warehoused metal because he could turn it over quickly, mostly to my Uncle Pope.

One morning at 7, he jumped out of bed and got dressed in a khaki uniform, emblazoned with the logo of a local copper distributor.

"What're you doing?" I asked. Tommy rarely got up before noon.

"Going to work." He retrieved a lunch pail I'd never seen before from the refrigerator.

"What now?"

He explained that he'd gotten a job on the loading dock of the copper company for the sole purpose of staking out the operation. "Twice a week, they get a train-car load of copper in. The load that's arriving the week after next is gonna be mine."

Tommy never ceased to amaze me. "You know, Tommy, if you concentrated your efforts on something legitimate, you'd make just as much money as you're making now, probably more."

"Yeah, but would I be having the fun?"

Without question, Tommy loved me and the boys, but after us, he loved to steal. It was a sickness, and it all went back to when some kid threw a rotten tomato at him when he was growing up.

Two weeks later, he stole the entire load of copper, fencing it to my Uncle Pope, and walking away with a $10,000 profit.

❊ ❊ ❊

I'd come home from shopping with the kids and see Tommy sitting in his favorite chair in the living room, smoking his pipe, scheming. This time he was watching television, something on the news about the high cost of mercury. I could almost hear the wheels turning. I waited until the kids were out of the room.

"Okay, what?" I said.

"A couple of dentists were just interviewed. They bitched about mercury tripling in price. They use it in fillings."

"So?"

"We know any dentists?"

"None that would buy hot mercury."

He smirked. "Everybody's greedy, Terri. If there's one thing you should've learned by now, it's that."

"Okay, so let's say you look in the yellow pages for crooked dentists, where are you going to get the mercury?"

"I'm a thief, that's what I do. I'll steal it."

❊ ❊ ❊

About a month later, Tommy came home with a metal box. He was handling it like it was filled with dynamite.

"Where are the kids?" he asked, his eyes never leaving the box.

"At my parents' house. What's in the box?" I was almost afraid to ask.

He placed it gingerly on the dining-room table

and carefully opened the lid. Resting neatly inside were nine plastic vials, each about the size of a shot glass, with gray liquid inside.

"You're looking at about twenty large worth of mercury," he said.

Unbelievable. He had gotten hold of a truck, forged bills of lading, went to a chemical company in the Bronx, and twenty minutes later drove out with the mercury. The guy was another Lex Luthor, a regular master criminal.

For the next week, we had more dentists at our house than I could count. Dentistry is one profession I thought would be relatively devoid of crooks, but I was obviously wrong. The next time you get a tooth crowned, consider that the gold might be booty from an armored car job.

Tommy cleared $9,000 on the mercury caper, but he wasn't about to rest on past triumphs. After that, it was one scam after another, one more ingenious than the next. While I chastised him for taking chances, I was awed at his ability to get away with it. We were living the good life, and to tell you the truth, I was enjoying the benefits, so much so that I'd closed up the wig business.

We had just finished dinner at a local Italian restaurant one evening when I asked, "So what's next on the hit parade?"

"What, you're intrigued? Tell me you don't want to get involved." Tommy was sucking on his pipe, annoying the party at the next table. They'd made comments, and he sneered at them, giving them his best George Raft imitation. They backed off. Tommy mumbled, "Citizens," in his vocabulary, a derogatory term.

"I don't. I was just wondering."

"That better be all you're doing," he said. "I do

the job, you do nothing but watch. So when I get busted–"

"Oh, Tommy."

"Hey, it's gotta happen. When I get busted, the cops come, you're in the clear." He would bend the rules one day by involving me in welfare fraud, but for now, he was a white knight.

Tommy considered jail time to be a consequence of his actions. "A criminal that doesn't expect to get caught sooner or later is an idiot. You've gotta figure time inside as part of the equation."

Tommy actually had a formula, figuring possible time in the slammer versus his profit to determine whether it was worth it financially to proceed with a scam. He calculated that a check- stealing caper he'd been planning for a while would be worth the effort.

❀ ❀ ❀

For months, Tommy had been trying to find an employee in the Wall Street community with a little larceny in his heart. Finally, with a tip from a bookie, he was given a line on a margin clerk at a big brokerage house who was into loan sharks for $15,000. With an 18 percent a week vigorish (interest), the total due was snowballing faster than the mark could keep up with payments. He needed a way to pay his debt or he'd be walking on crutches for the foreseeable future.

Tommy met with the clerk. He told him that he was now going to funnel selected checks to Tommy instead of to account holders. At first, the clerk balked, but he had little choice but to comply. Tommy told me how the scam would work.

"Dickhead gives me a check that's due a client of the brokerage for say, $50,000. I give the check to

Pope before it's reported stolen, he cashes it through a crooked banker he knows using phony ID to match the name on the check. Once it's cashed, the banker can say 'Oops.'"

"What's your end?"

"Twenty for me, twenty for your uncle, five each to the banker and the clerk."

"You expect to get away with this?"

"For a while."

"What's that supposed to mean?"

"Figure we can do a few checks, varying amounts, before we get bagged. I'll make about a hundred large, do a year in the can."

The price of doing business, according to Tommy Ernst.

❊   ❊   ❊

One bright sunny morning, I was in the yard with the twins when my Uncle Pope's car screeched to a halt in front of the house. He flew out and barreled up to me.

"Where's Tommy?"

I got out of earshot of the boys. "Sleeping," I said, more than a little worried. "What's going on?"

"Go in the house, get his ass out of bed."

I did what I was told and practically dragged a groggy Tommy into the yard in his underwear.

"Hey, Pope, what's up?" he said, his eyes barely open.

"What's up is my man at the bank couldn't get the last check all the way through the system before it was reported stolen."

"So? We got paid, fuck him."

My uncle stood there slack jawed. "What do you mean, fuck him? I don't believe you. We gotta give him the money back."

This was a big check, Tommy had cleared $25,000.

Tommy looked at Pope like he had three heads. "Hey, I'm a thief, I don't give money back."

❊   ❊   ❊

Tommy gave the money back. So much for words to live by. My uncle was very persuasive. For now, the crisis had passed, but the FBI was on the case, and Tommy expected to get busted any day. He was pissed, to say the least. Not angry, mind you, because he was probably going to jail, but mad because he'd only made $70,000 of his projected $100,000. To Tommy's way of thinking, $100,000 was worth a year in jail, but $70,000, no way.

"I'll figure out a way to make up the thirty large," he said and calmly sat down in his favorite living-room chair, opened a book, and waited for the good guys to come and arrest him.

He didn't have long to wait.

Three days later, while I was preparing breakfast, two FBI agents showed up on our doorstep. Fortunately, we'd had the presence of mind to pack the kids off to Wild Acres for an extended visit with their great-grandmother. Tommy was in the shower.

I answered the door holding a coffeepot. "Yes?"

The two guys looked like clones. Before either one said anything, I knew they were FBI. Both were blank faced and tense. This was the tail end of J. Edgar Hoover's reign in the Bureau when all the agents dressed alike in dark suits and ties, had white hankies peeking exactly one inch out of their breast pockets, and had tennis-ball haircuts. They also wore signature narrow-brimmed hats.

One suit showed me his credentials. Their names are forever lost to ancient history, but the banter went something like this: "Special Agent Ballbag, FBI. This is Special Agent Hungwell. We've got an arrest warrant for Thomas Ernst and a search warrant for the premises. And you would be?"

The FBI had paid frequent visits to my parents' house when I was a teenager (and privy to what was going on), both to lock up my father and to search the premises. They knew that wiseguys never resisted arrest. They'd wait patiently for my father to pack a small bag, finish washing the car, or whatever else he had to do. But when they searched the house, they would invariably make a mess, much to my mother's chagrin. Of course, they'd never find anything, either.

I was determined not to have my house demolished.

"I would be Terri Dee, Tommy's wife." Telling them that I was Tommy's wife was easier than trying to explain our living arrangement.

Agent Hungwell said, "You related to John Dee?"

"I'm his daughter."

They relaxed a bit. "Mr. Ernst around?"

"Upstairs in the shower. He's expecting you. You guys had breakfast?"

They looked at each other. Agent Ballbag said, "Not really."

"Tell you what...c'mon in. I'll make you something to eat, and we'll talk. My husband'll be down in about twenty minutes." I went upstairs and told Tommy that we had the FBI for company.

"I'll pack," he said and went back to shaving.

I took their hats, showed them to the kitchen, made a pile of scrambled eggs, bacon, Italian bread toast, and a new pot of coffee. They enjoyed the food and were very polite. Before Tommy made his appearance, I asked them if I could accompany them through the house as they searched, open drawers, empty closets, and be of any help I could.

"I remember when I was a teenager, at my parents', you guys would make a big mess. I'd rather not have that here, okay?"

I was told that it would be no problem.

Tommy joined us for breakfast. Everyone was friendly, no harsh words or intimidation. One big happy family.

It took the agents two hours to search the house under my supervision. Naturally, they found nothing incriminating. Tommy stayed in the living room. After the search, the agents gave Tommy and me a few minutes alone. I cried, he was stoic. While I was expecting him to be busted, it still came as a bit of a shock knowing he'd be out of my life for a while.

The place was neat as a pin when they led Tommy away in cuffs. They even apologized for any inconvenience that they may have caused.

"No problem," I said, "I'm sure you'll be back someday."

"No doubt."

❋   ❋   ❋

Tommy was sentenced to one year. Prior to his going away, he took out a three-year, $18,000 personal loan, which I would live on. We thought it wise not to have any unexplained income while he was gone, and I agreed to stay away from the cash reserves. Since the demise of the wig business, I was totally dependent on him, so it had to look like I was living frugally, now that he was in the can and not earning any money.

I acclimated. The kids kept me busy, and I spent time at my parents' house. Tommy was originally charged with a federal crime, but the state eventually got the case, and he wound up doing his time in Clinton Penitentiary upstate. With time off for the good behavior, he would undoubtedly embrace, he'd be home in about ten months.

The time went surprisingly fast. I visited him twice a month, flying up in a chartered plane rather than making the nine-hour drive. A friend owned the plane and was willing to wait until Tommy got out to get paid. I knew our finances were being scrutinized, so I lived off the loan money and only dipped into the cash reserve sparingly.

Three weeks prior to his release, Tommy was transferred to Riker's Island in New York City, which made visiting him much more convenient. He had just days to go when one of his friends stopped by the house. Mickey was a mob gofer, one of Tommy's googans, who did odd jobs for him and anyone else who needed a petty criminal on short notice. Tall, in his early thirties, he was another guy who fancied himself a lady's man.

He said he wanted to talk to me about something important, so I invited him in. All he wanted was to get laid. Within minutes, he was all over me. I had to threaten to tell Tommy before he let up.

"Tommy?" he sneered. "He was getting his on the side before he went away. What's good for him oughta be good for you, too."

"What are you talking about?"

"He was banging Angel, Paulie's wife, for months. C'mon, you hadda know."

Angel was married to Paul Messina, the margin clerk who had worked the check-cashing scam with Tommy. Paul had been convicted before Tommy and was in jail for three months before Tommy even came to trial. He was still in. Tommy had mentioned

Angel's name in passing; nothing struck me as suspicious at the time. I didn't want to believe Mickey, but before I condemned Tommy, I had to do a little investigating.

I showed Mickey the door and checked the phone book. The Messinas lived in Elcenville, a small community on the other side of Staten Island. I dialed the number and hung up when a woman answered. If I broke the land-speed record, I could be there in ten minutes.

During the ride, I experienced a rainbow of emotions: hate, fear, jealousy, rage, hurt. But without the facts, I didn't know what to believe. If Tommy had been any other man, I would've believed the accusation and chalked it up to the Asshole Syndrome, a malady suffered by most men at least once in their lives. But I felt that Tommy was different. The two years we'd been back together had been the happiest of my life. We rarely argued, the kids seemed happy and secure, and Tommy treated me like a lady. The last thing I would suspect was him cheating on me. I had to know.

I took a deep breath and knocked on the door of the aluminum-sided house. A short, dumpy brunette wearing a shapeless housedress answered. She had pretty eyes, I gave her that.

"Yes?" she said.

"Angel?"

"Yes? Do I know you?"

"You may know my boyfriend, Tommy Ernst."

The color drained from her face. Now I knew. Tommy *had* cheated on me. I pushed past her. "I'm coming in."

There was a middle-aged woman sitting on a sofa in the living room watching television. She glanced up at me and said, "Hi." I ignored her and turned on Angel, who was right behind me.

"Did you have sex with Tommy? Yes or no."

She began shaking her head like she had palsy. "No, no."

I took a step toward her until I was practically in her face. "You're lying. Don't lie to me or you'll be sorry."

The woman on the couch got up. "Hey, who—"

I whirled on her. "Shut the fuck up, and sit down." Little Tiger was now Big Tiger, and she was pissed. Back to Angel. "Well?"

Angel raised her hands as if to protect herself. "Look, Tommy came over here one day to give me some money, money he owed Paulie. We had a couple of drinks, one thing led to another. It was only one time, I swear."

I hauled off and hit her in the nose with everything I had. Her head snapped back and blood sprayed everywhere. She went down. I was right on top of her, pummeling her face with my fists until I exhausted myself. Her friend on the sofa didn't move a muscle.

Angel's face was a bloody pulp. She was whimpering as I got off her. "Keep your fucking hands off other women's men." I stormed out of the house.

Back in the car, I began to tremble. I didn't know if my rage was directed more at Tommy, who wasn't available for a confrontation, or at Angel for screwing him. As my anger subsided, I considered my next move. When I was in control enough to drive, I eased the car into gear and headed for my next port of call: Riker's Island.

❋ ❋ ❋

I parked my car in the visitors' parking area and

took the shuttle bus to the jail where Tommy was housed. The visiting room was a windowless affair, separated by a floor-to-ceiling barrier of wire-reinforced glass with heavy wooden picnic benches on either side. The prisoner and visitor communicate by telephone; there was no physical contact.

Tommy was all smiles when a corrections officer ushered him in and took a place behind him. Tommy's smile vanished when he saw me. We each picked up a phone.

"Hi, babe," he said.

"Did you screw Angel Messina?" Right to the point.

He looked at me like I was crazy. "Me? No way. She's a pig."

I was deeply hurt. I had been certain that Tommy had been faithful to me. Now that confidence was shattered. Up until today, I had also been certain that he hadn't lied to me. I was enraged.

I bellowed, "You sonofabitch!" and began smashing the phone against the supposedly shatterproof glass. It spider webbed, but held. Tommy dropped his phone and jumped from his chair. Now, without the benefit of a phone, his calming words were muffled.

"Calm down?" I screeched. "You motherfucker!" I upended the bench and looked for something else to destroy. At that point, three corrections officers came into the room and told me to simmer down. They directed me to a waiting room that was used by Riker's Island supervisors to greet visiting politicos and other big shots.

"Get me on a bus. I want out of here!" I yelled. They probably thought I was a nut case. I was a mess. Throwing a tantrum takes a lot out of a person. One officer told me that if I calmed down, they'd personally put me on a bus and get me the hell off the island.

"Wait here a few minutes, I'll check the bus schedule," one of the COs said. He left and the other two boogied out right behind him. Apparently no one wanted to stay with the crazy broad.

While they were gone, the rage returned. In the center of the room, there was an elaborate scaled-down display of the Riker's Island facility. Someone had taken a lot of time and energy to put the model together. I decided to destroy it. By the time the COs returned, the display looked like it had been nuked.

This was the early 1970s. There wasn't a female detention facility on Riker's. The COs simply didn't know what to do with me, so they ushered me off the island and to my car via radio car, lights flashing and siren blasting.

The day Tommy was released, I got a bill for $11,000 in damages. I still haven't paid it.

❋   ❋   ❋

Tommy came clean, admitting to his fling with Angel. He swore on my kids that it was the only time he'd strayed. By that time my wrath had been satiated; I had the bill for damages to prove it. And besides, I loved the guy. I wasn't about to throw him out for one mistake.

We settled back into our routine. Tommy's first order of business was to make up the $30,000 he felt he'd lost as a result of the early bust in the stolen-check scam.

"Jesus, Tommy, are you still on that?"

"You bet your ass. I've got an idea."

"What else is new?"

On paper, Tommy had me rent him the down-stairs apartment in our home. We weren't married, he reasoned, had two different last names—the makings of the perfect welfare swindle. Tommy received a welfare rent check every month because he claimed that he was unemployed and couldn't afford the rent. In those days, the welfare people took your word for it. The checks would eventually make up for the money he claimed he was shorted. Tommy had to work a scam to be happy. Now he was happy, but it was the first time that I was actively involved in a crime. Meanwhile, Tommy was still running his Sheetrock business and attending to other illegal ventures.

Just before it all came crashing down, Tommy managed to get the master keys for every Cadillac ever made. We literally drove a new (stolen) Cadillac every week for months. After a week, he'd sell the car to my Uncle Mike, who switched VIN numbers and shipped the vehicle overseas.

Without fail, every Monday as Tommy was leaving the house, he'd ask me what color Caddy I wanted for that week. After a while, we ran out of colors, so I'd make up outlandish ones.

"Get a puce one this week."

"Right." In two hours he'd be back with a black Cadillac. "Couldn't find puce. Is that a real color?"

※　※　※

The day the slide began I had come home to find the front door locked, something neither Tommy nor I ever did. We lived in a safe area. Besides, every burglar on the Island knew who my father was. They burgled a wide path around our house.

After letting myself in, I walked through an eerily quiet house. Our dog, a massive German shepherd, was kept tethered by a chain in the kitchen when the house was empty because he was prone to attacking strangers. When I entered the kitchen, I saw a naked chain. No dog.

"Tommy?"

No answer. The kids were in school, but Tommy was supposed to be home.

"Tommy?"

Still no answer. Now I was getting worried.

I called his name again from the foot of the stairs leading to the second floor.

"Up here," Tommy said, his voice a harsh whisper.

Tommy was in our bedroom, sitting on the floor facing the door. The dog was lying at his feet. The shades were drawn.

"What the hell's going on?" I asked. Not since the time he'd accidentally broken my nose when we were kids had I seen Tommy Ernst shaken. But he quickly shifted gears and got cocky.

"The Bilottis are looking for me. I'm gonna have to lay on some bullshit to get myself out of a jam."

For the next few days, Tommy would be a walking dead man. Later, when he was murdered right in front of me, I'd lost the love of my life, and I didn't want to go on without him. But before I crumpled up and died, I was going to exact revenge. Soon I would realize that I almost made a costly mistake, but I was adrift, and my life would slowly circle the drain until I entered an abyss from which I knew I might never return.

7 Curse of the Dead Pussy

ather Dominic Petrucci, the pastor at St. Sylvester's, peered at me over the top of his reading glasses. Obviously embarrassed, he said, "I'm sorry, Terri, we can't hold a funeral Mass for Tommy here."

We were in the rectory. It was a warm spring day, but it could have been the middle of winter as far as I was concerned. Tommy had been killed the day before, and I was a mental case.

My father had graciously volunteered to handle the funeral arrangements, but I had insisted on doing it. In spite of my mental state, which was fragile, I felt that keeping busy was the best therapy.

I was confused. We belonged to the parish and were active in its affairs. "Why not? Is it scheduling...something else?" I let my voice trail off.

The priest struggled for the right words. "Uh, it was a killing, Terri, a mob killing. We don't condone—"

I pushed myself to the edge of my chair. "You don't condone? Tommy's dead. Our family is active in this church. We contribute, attend Mass every week, us and the kids. Tommy was an altar boy here. You don't condone? You've got some nerve!" I was getting hot. Priest or no priest, the good father was going to get a piece of my mind.

He got up from behind his desk, his hands raised in a conciliatory gesture. "Now, Terri...."

I was on my feet. "Now Terri, my ass! My Tommy gets a Mass here, or you get one!" I was sorry as soon as I'd said it, but there was no taking back that I'd just threatened a priest. He just stood there and stared at me. Finally I said, "Look, Father, I'm sorry."

He sat back down, shaking his head. "This isn't my doing, Terri. I've got parishioners to answer to, the archdiocese."

We went back and forth for almost an hour. There was no budging him. Finally, I thanked him for his time and left.

There was the typical crowd of Italian mourners at my parents' house. Wakes got them out in droves, whether they knew the deceased or not. There were two old ladies sitting together in the living room crying their eyes out. Neither of them had ever met Tommy. I knew them to be professional mourners; every Italian neighborhood has them. No matter who dies, whether they knew them or not, they turn out at the wake and funeral and wail like they've lost a child. Once, when I was a kid, I saw one old lady try to drag a corpse out of the coffin. Scared the hell out of me. She kept on screaming, "Angelo! Angelo! Why did God take you?" Turns out Angelo was in the next room, but it mattered little.

My father hooked my arm and gently guided me from the crowd in the kitchen, ground zero for any Italian wake. In the relative quiet of a hallway, he said, "The church thing's been taken care of."

"What church thing?" I could barely get the words out. I hadn't slept in thirty-six hours. The last time I'd eaten was a distant memory.

"The priest, what's his name...Petrucci? He had a change of heart. The funeral Mass is on Wednesday."

"What did you do?" I had a vision of my Uncle Pope and Uncle Mike paying the priest a visit with swinging baseball bats.

My father smirked. "You know how much I give to that church every year? It's always about money." He squeezed my arm. "I know you loved him, Tiger. You come to me for anything you need, you and the kids, okay?"

"Thanks, Daddy."

✳ ✳ ✳

My boys were scheduled to stay at a relative's house that night. I thought it better to have them away from the stress of a houseful of mourners. As they were getting their stuff together, I went to the garage to get the car out.

I was still in a daze, but had eaten and felt a little better. As I entered the darkened garage, I smelled a strange odor, but couldn't pin it down. I gave it no further thought, opened the door on the Caddy, and slid in. I mean I really slid in. The seat was wet with something slick. I thought that perhaps one of the kids had spilled a soda and put my hand on the leather to investigate. It came up bloody.

I let out a muted gasp and jumped out of the car, my heart in my mouth. The garage was in semi-darkness. I identified the odor as fresh blood. Was someone in the garage with me? I backed away from the car and flipped the switch. The garage flooded with piercing fluorescent light.

I looked around. I was definitely alone. Sweat ran down my spine as I inched back toward the car and looked inside. The front seat was streaked with blood, a lot of it. I looked in the backseat for a body. Empty. I stuck my head inside the car. Wedged into the passenger foot well was a mutilated and very dead cat.

I could hear the muffled voices of my family inside the house. As I was deciding what to do, my son, John, waltzed into the garage.

"We ready to go, Mom?" He crinkled his nose. "What's that smell?"

"Go back inside the house, John. Tell grandpa to come out here."

He advanced toward the car. "What's going on?"

"Get in the house!" Tears erupted. I tried to hold them back. Lost cause. "Go on," I said gently now, "get grandpa."

He retreated without another word.

As soon as my father entered the garage, he smelled the blood. "What's inside?"

"Dead cat."

His face hardened. "Motherfuckers." He looked at the carnage. "A message."

"A message? What message? I sleep with the cats?" I wasn't thinking very clearly.

My father was embarrassed. He averted his eyes from mine. "You talk, you're a dead pussy."

"Huh? Talk about what?"

"Whoever whacked Tommy did this. They think you can identify the shooter."

"The guy had a ski mask on, for God's sake. I could tell you how tall he was, that's about it."

"Yeah," my father said, "but why take chances? Someone's telling you to keep your mouth shut."

I sat down heavily on a metal stool. My first

thought was of my kids. The thought of not seeing them grow up horrified me. "Now I've got this to worry about?"

My father ran his hands through his hair. "Let me think." Seconds later he said, "I'll spread the word that you know nothing, you'll say nothing. It'll get back to whoever did this. In the meantime, Joey Maniscalco will be your second skin."

Maniscalco was a rough customer, but he was loyal to my family. He was an extremely violent man who would do literally anything for money. He once beat the crap out of the father of the bride, pulling the man from his daughter's arms as they danced to "Daddy's Little Girl" at the wedding reception because he owed Joey money from a gambling debt. He did this in front of three hundred witnesses. No one saw anything. An unlucky gambler himself, he was always broke. He was known on the street as Joey Funzalo.

Think about it.

He wound up sleeping on my couch for two weeks, cradling a sawed-off shotgun. When I left the house, he was right behind me. My kids were shipped off to grandma in Jersey. Screw school. I wasn't going to have them around in case there was an attempt on my life.

After three weeks, my father deemed me safe from harm. "The word's out, Tiger. You're okay." Joey was cut loose. My kids came home.

❋　❋　❋

The wake was a blur. Literally thousands of people attended. The Bilotti brothers were conspicuous by their absence, but I was too distraught to give a damn. Not until the day of the funeral did my grief begin to give way to anger.

The FBI was camped on the roof of a restaurant across from the funeral home. As Tommy's casket was carried to the hearse for the short drive to the church, one agent nearly fell off the roof snapping pictures. I was dressed all in black, complete with veil and gloves. I ceremoniously removed one and gave the rooftop voyeurs the finger. They waved back.

My children took Tommy's death very hard. He was the first man in my life who had treated them with dignity and was devoid of conventional vices. As I gathered the kids in my arms, waiting for the driver of my limousine to open the door for us, my mother, slightly drunk, sidled alongside me.

"You know, Terri," she said cheerily, "you look like Jackie Kennedy standing here, all in black, with the kids."

I swear, if she wasn't my mother, I would have decked her.

❈ ❈ ❈

No matter how many condolences I got at the funeral, no matter the number of pledges of unselfish support and the promises to "keep in touch" or "call me for anything you need," when the pomp and ghoulishness of the ceremony was over, I went home with my children to resume my life. After things settled down, my women friends would keep their husbands away from me because now I was viewed as a possible competitor. Tommy's friends would vanish forever because most of them owed him money and they had gotten away clean. But I had my kids; thank God I had my kids. And I also had something else to keep me going–revenge.

As I sat in my empty bedroom, peeling off the last of my mourning clothes, fighting the desire to ball them into an unrecognizable knot and burn them, I began plotting the end of Tommy and Joey Bilotti.

There was no doubt in my mind that they had murdered Tommy, if not by themselves, then by using some up-and-coming wiseguy who wanted to make his bones. I told no one about my emerging plans to kill them—not my family, not my best friend Margo, no one. The more I visualized their deaths, the better I felt. Blood lust had no better definition.

My weapon of choice was a gun, although I would rather have used a knife to get up close and personal to watch the fear and pain in their eyes as life slowly ebbed away. But I knew that I would have to kill them at the same time, and a knife was impractical. I was nothing if not practical. If one of the brothers managed to get away, I might as well turn the weapon on myself because I'd be a walking dead person. There would be nowhere I could hide. I wasn't so much worried about myself as I was concerned for my kids. They deserved to have their mother around, warts and all.

The day after the funeral, while I was contemplating a way to get a gun that wouldn't broadcast to the world that I was on the warpath, my father called me.

"You see today's *Daily News?*"

I told him I hadn't.

"Joey Gallo got whacked last night, right in his own backyard."

Joey "Crazy Joe" Gallo was a rebel in the New York mob. Reputed to be one of the shooters who murdered Albert Anastasia along with "Chin" Gigante, he had languished in mob limbo, never getting his due for a job well done, at least according to him. He operated on his own, with the help of his brother and a few of the fringe element and cast-aways from the other families. Gallo was shot, my father told me, in front of his fiancé and another couple (the actor, Jerry Orbach and his wife) while dining in Umberto's Clam House in Little Italy as they celebrated their engagement. An unwritten rule in the mob was that you never killed someone in front of family, and you certainly didn't do it in Little Italy, the Mafia's demilitarized zone. That was like Dr. Ruth playing for the Knicks. Wouldn't happen. Someone was sending a message.

I suspected that my father was telling me about Gallo's death for a good reason, other than spreading the news about "family" business.

"Interesting," I said, "but we didn't deal with Gallo. Or did we?"

"We didn't, Tiger, but maybe Tommy did."

"What's that supposed to mean?"

"Rumors, Tiger, rumors. Word on the street is that Tommy and Crazy Joe were talking serious talk."

"About what?" My heart sank at the mention of Tommy's name.

"I don't know, but maybe it bears looking into." He sighed. "Look, Tiger, I know you're pissed. I'd be, too. But if you're thinking you're gonna do something about Tommy's murder, I'm gonna have to tell you to stop thinking about it."

My father knew me, knew the wild, uncontrollable me. He would know of my overwhelming desire to inflict pain on the Bilotti brothers. "You can't stop me."

"Oh yes I can, and I will. I'm not about to lose a daughter to something as useless as revenge. If it was the Bilottis did Tommy, it was business. You accept it and move on."

"I can't do that."

"That's what I figured." He changed direction. "You remember that old detective, used to come to the house? Jimmy Shea, his name was, ate dinner with us every now and then?"

I had a glimmer of recognition. A fat, red-faced Irishman, on my father's payroll like a lot of cops. But I remember they seemed to genuinely like each other. Lots of laughing over drinks in my father's den. "Yeah, I remember."

"He used to tell me, he'd say, 'You know what separates a good cop from a bad one?' And I'd say, what? He'd tell me, 'The ability to keep an open mind.' That guy caught more really bad guys than McGarrett on *Hawaii Five-0*. I mean really bad guys, not us. You know how he did it?"

"How?"

"I remember one case when all his cop buddies zeroed in on a junkie with a piss-poor motive for murder and wouldn't look anywhere else. But Shea, he kept an open mind and wound up locking up the guy's wife. Got a conviction, too. You know what I'm saying?"

I was about to become a good cop.

※　※　※

Over the course of the next two weeks, bodies began to drop. Seven total, all associates of Joey Gallo, found in conspicuous locations, tortured and mutilated. More messages. The newspapers quoted anonymous police sources as saying the murders were a result of an internal struggle for power. Well, no kidding, I thought, but the sheer number of victims in such a short time spelled something more than the typical dick-measuring contest among mobsters.

I could have asked my father to put out some feelers, find out what was going on, but I was afraid that too many questions would attract the people who were doing the shooting and possibly add his name to the list of victims. I decided on an age-old approach.

I had Margo watch the kids one night while I got dolled up for a fact-finding mission.

"Out trolling?" she asked as she watched me apply the finishing touches to my makeup.

"You know me better than that. Tommy's dead three weeks." I slipped into my coat. "The kids are in the back watching television."

"So where're you going?"

"Off to be a good cop."

※ ※ ※

I hit Little Italy in Lower Manhattan like a hot broad looking to score with a wiseguy. Like entertainers, gangsters had their share of groupies, and that night I became one. I intended to zero in on the young Turks who were full of themselves and the lifestyle. They liked to talk, liked to impress swooning women with their toughness and power.

The Red Rose Bar & Grill on Elizabeth Street, right down the block from the Fifth Precinct station house, was a magnet for mobsters, cops, judges, and celebrities. I was unknown there, but I'd heard my father mention it more than a few times. ("Best Italian food outside of my mother's kitchen.") Where there's good food, there's wiseguys. It's a given.

That night, the place was jammed. Manhattan's criminal court and the jail, ominously known as the Tombs, were a mere two blocks away, and that attracted the cops and lawyers. They held court at one end of the bar while the handful of neighborhood wiseguys bellied up to the other end. Jackie

Gleason was there, too, with an entourage of women, sitting in a circular booth in the back. In the short time that I was there, he got so drunk he fell on his ass while trying to find the men's room. When he and his escorts left, they were immediately mobbed at the door by neighborhood kids. Gleason, it seemed, had a habit of handing out dollar bills to local kids. That night he couldn't find his wallet with both hands, so one of the women in his group did the honors.

Two wiseguys zoned in on me right away. They introduced themselves as Handsome Tony and Louie the Jew. Tony wasn't handsome, and Louie wasn't Jewish, but they were both blabbermouths. Within two hours, I had the scoop on Tommy's killing. Play hard to get with a drunk and after a while he'll tell you his family's secrets. Now I was hearing confessions in stereo about the kind of family I was most interested in.

Just prior to his murder, Joey Gallo had done a few years in an upstate prison. Always the innovator, and a little bit of a whack job, he devised a plan to take over the five New York crime families. He began to recruit black prisoners who were about to be released as part of a new gang that would kill the heads of the families. Once accomplished, he would reign supreme as the king of the New York underworld.

Tommy was in on the plan from day one and was promised a top position in Gallo's new regime. To kick off his campaign, Gallo recruited some brain-damaged black man to kill crime boss Joe Columbo at a rally in Columbus Circle while he spoke before a group of 5,000 people protesting FBI harassment of Italian Americans. Columbo was surrounded by bodyguards, and there were enough undercover FBI personnel and New York City cops in the crowd to start their own police department.

The gunman managed to get off one shot, severely wounding Columbo, before he was killed in a fusillade of bullets that no one ever claimed credit for firing. Columbo lingered for years in a semicoma before dying.

Immediately after the shooting, the five families joined forces and cleaned house. Everyone connected with the plot was eliminated.

"Ernst was one of them," Louie said as he made one more attempt at grabbing my ass. I brushed his hand away.

"This guy Ernst a friend of yours?" Tony asked.

"Someone I knew," I said, barely able to keep my last drink down. I'd almost condemned the Bilottis to death without knowing the facts. I was beginning to wonder if my father hadn't known the truth all along, reasoning that if he told me what really happened, I probably wouldn't have believed him, thinking he'd made up the story to sway me from killing the Bilottis.

I was deflated. Planning revenge had kept me going. Without it, I felt empty, useless to avenge Tommy's death.

I left without another word. I had to get on with my life.

❊ ❊ ❊

Tommy had a little more than $80,000 in cash squirreled away in a safe deposit box. I was a signatory and had no trouble getting to the money. I lived off it for a while, but soon got restless. The longer I stayed at home, the more depressed I got. The aura of Tommy was everywhere, and I knew that I had to get out of the house or lose my mind. I decided that a job was out of the question. I had proven entrepreneurial skills and didn't want to waste my time making money for someone else. A home-based business was also out; the less time I spent in the house, the better. Therefore, going back into the wig business, no matter how successful I knew I would be, was discounted.

I was determined to keep my kids out of harm's way. The dead cat in my car was still fresh in my mind. I wanted to live a clean life, run an honest business, to start over again.

I decided to go into the bar business. I knew next to nothing about how to run a successful bar, but I'd spent most of my adult life drinking in them, and I was sure I'd be a fast learner.

I began looking for a job as a bartender, just to get some experience in the day-to-day operation of the business. I'd watched bartenders long enough to be able to make any drink in my sleep. The Pussycat Cafe in Manhattan had an advertisement in the *Daily News*. I showed up the next day dressed in my next-to-sleaziest outfit. The real deal would have gotten me arrested.

The place was packed at three in the afternoon. It seems that they got the overflow from Jilly's, a famous New York watering hole, located down the block. The crowd consisted of all men, dressed in the same style gray business suit. I hesitated as I entered the place, thinking that maybe I should open up a gray suit store in the neighborhood and clean up. But I was intrigued and asked the grizzled old bartender for the owner.

"You ever tend bar before?" the owner, who said his name was Sol, asked. He was short, somewhere between sixty and death, with a pasty white, jowly face that looked like a collapsed soufflé. A foot-long cigar was stuck between yellow teeth.

"Some," I lied.

He looked me up and down. "Maybe we can use you for other things. You drink?"

"Yeah," I said, "you buying?" I didn't like this guy. He made me nervous.

He smirked. "No, but other people will. Listen, you come here every night at eight, stay till closing, sit at the bar, and have guys buy you drinks. You get a cut, plus half a yard."

I was already putting on my coat. "I didn't apply for a job as a B-girl. You want a bartender, I'm it. I'll increase your business." I jerked a thumb over my shoulder. "I'm sure your customers would rather look at me than Father Time over there."

He contemplated my proposal. "Tell you what...I'll put you on for one day a week...Fridays. I gotta keep Tony, he's like the commode, a fixture. But the Friday guy's a schmuck, probably stealing more than he's taking in. Sound okay?"

I was in. The job was ideal. I could learn the business with a minimal amount of hours invested, and working during the day would have me home with my kids at night.

During the next two months, I learned more about how to cheat customers than a carnival barker could have taught me.

My lessons began on the first day. I reported promptly at 11 AM, learned the layout of the bar, got my bank counted, and was ready for the first customer when the doors opened at 11:30. As soon as I poured my first drink, Sol motioned to me from the other side of the room.

I made my way to where he was sitting. "Sit down, kid."

I sat.

"You're pouring too much booze."

The guy had eyes like a goddamn eagle. The room was so dimly lit that you needed a seeing-eye dog to get to the john.

"What are you talking about? I poured from a shot glass."

"Yeah, but you did it in the wrong order." He explained that instead of pouring the booze over ice and then adding the mixer, I was to put the ice and mixer in the glass first, then add the liquor. "Fill up the glass with soda, just a splash of booze."

I rolled my eyes. "You're the boss."

"You bet your ass I am. And oh yeah, no swizzle sticks. If they can't mix the drinks, the booze stays on top. Tastes stronger."

The liquor was watered down, but not the stuff in the well or the bottom-shelf bottles. This was the cheap booze, the crap that tasted like turpentine. Adding water to that junk wouldn't matter, it was high profit to begin with. Sol doctored the good stuff and paid off the State Liquor Authority inspectors when he got caught.

If anyone bought me a drink, I drank iced tea poured from a Chivas Regal Scotch bottle. Sol was so cheap that he hung the paper towel dispensers in the bathrooms at eye level so customers would only grab a few towels to dry their hands because water would drip down their arms due to the height of the dispenser.

After a few months, I'd had it. I cornered Sol after a shift.

"I quit."

He almost swallowed his cigar. I'd doubled the amount of customer traffic on Fridays. He'd been asking me for a month to work nights. I'd always begged off, using my kids as an excuse.

"What do you mean you quit? Why?"

"Because you're a thief." The businessmen who frequented the Pussycat were working stiffs. Their bosses bellied up to the bar at Jilly's. We got the guys who worked for their money. I hated to see them get cheated.

He seemed perplexed. "Okay, but why do you want to quit?"

❋ ❋ ❋

The next joint I worked in was Emily's on Staten Island. I'd learned how to cheat customers at the Pussycat Cafe, which meant that I also learned how to watch for cheating bartenders. Now that I knew that aspect of the business, I wanted to find a legitimate place where I could learn ordering, stock, payroll, and food preparation. Emily's fit the bill.

It was a neighborhood joint on Staten Island owned by an honest woman in her thirties. She treated her customers fairly, poured a decent drink for a good price, and went out of her way to run a clean kitchen. Her customers were mostly guys, neighborhood family men who bent an elbow after work or stopped in for lunch.

A few days after I began tending bar, I took a sailor's holiday and stopped in for a few drinks after a wedding I'd attended. I was dressed formally and stuck out like a Klan member at an NAACP meeting. But I knew everyone in the bar and didn't feel out of place. Sitting at the other end of the bar was a man dressed in a tuxedo. What are the odds? The last person to be dressed formally in Emily's was dragged out of his own coffin from the funeral home next door to reign at his own Irish wake.

The gentleman bought me a drink and slid over to where I was sitting. His name was Tony DeLorenzo, and at six four with dark hair, he looked a little like Walter Matthau in his younger days.

As soon as he sat next to me, I said, "Okay, I'll marry you."

He looked at me like I was crazy, but laughed anyway. "What's that supposed to mean?

"A friend of mine tells me that I don't date, I get married."

He looked frightened.

"Do you?"

I squeezed his arm and laughed. "The last thing I need is another husband."

He seemed relieved.

Three months later we were married.

❃ ❃ ❃

Tony was a good man, and more importantly, he wasn't mobbed up. He owned a few hotels in Miami and was always in a good mood, always ready with a joke, never afraid to act a little goofy in order to get a laugh. He got along with everyone, including my kids and my parents. I checked for a dark side, but couldn't find any. I felt safe with Tony, which was a mistake I seemed to make with all my men. His betrayal would be particularly painful.

❃ ❃ ❃

After three months behind the stick in Emily's, I was ready for a place of my own. One thing I had discovered about the bar business was that the owner had to be there all the time, which was impossible, or the employees would become de facto partners. Almost everyone steals in the bar business. I knew that I needed a good honest partner to cut my losses. Enter Nicki Rogers.

Nicki was a regular at Emily's. About my age, thirty-seven, Nicki was big, strong as the proverbial ox, a former stripper, and very gay. She was also

honest and had a good reputation in the neighborhood.

My cousin Charlie had told me about a shuttered
bar in the Stapleton section of the Island. With a little renovation, I envisioned a nice neighborhood
joint, not unlike what Emily had on the other side of
town.

One night I posed the question to Nicki over a
few drinks at Emily's. "You want to go into the bar
business with me? Fifty-fifty partners."

"How much money do I need?"

"Five thousand, maybe a little more after we fix
the place up." I told her where the old bar was located. "We can take a ride tomorrow, check it out. You
have $5,000?"

She downed a beer with one gulp. "Nope, but I
know where I can get it."

"Where?"

"From a guy I'm seeing."

"I thought you're a lesbian."

"Every day except Saturday." she said. "That's
the day he can get away from his wife. He's loaded;
I have incentive."

Nicki got the money from her boyfriend. She
couldn't have her name on the liquor license, however, because she'd taken a bust for writing a bad
check when she was a teenager. She trusted me to
be square with her even though she appeared
nowhere in the business filings. She was the best
partner anyone could ever have. Thirty years later,
we're still friends.

It took some doing to get the liquor license
because the Dalessio name was notorious. A lawyer
finally secured the license after six months of bat-
tling the SLA.

We were in business.

8 Stand Up, Sit Down

"What you've got here," my father said, "is a gay bar."

It was a Friday night. We'd been in business about four months. The place was jammed. Nicki was behind the stick, and my father had stopped in to check on his vending machines. We were customers like everyone else, and he'd come around once a week or so, order a club soda, and leave a fifty on the bar. Still doing his PR routine, still making the rounds.

It was true that Nicki had her lesbian following, but lately, more and more gay men were stopping by. We'd turned into a gay bar all right, but only at night. During the day, we had the neighborhood crowd and the obligatory contingent of wiseguys.

"So?" I said. "They spend money like everyone else. Probably more."

"My point exactly," my father said above the din. "You should take advantage of it."

"How?"

"Advertise."

"What for? They're packed in already."

"There's always room for more business."

True enough. We had a mandated capacity that was ignored because we took care of the local precinct.

The next day, I took out ads in two Greenwich Village newspapers, inviting the entire gay world to *"Bill Bailey's."* Nicki and I had been stuck for a name up until a few weeks before opening. We decided on *Bill Bailey's* when we heard Bobby Darin's song of the same name on the radio.

❋   ❋   ❋

The ads worked wonders. On weekends we had a line of customers that stretched around the block. Within a month, we instituted a gay review featuring drag queens and go-go boys. The neighbors loved us.

My waitresses were either transvestites or transsexuals. My best waitress was Michelle, a transsexual. I would defy anyone to make Michelle as a former male. She was absolutely stunning, a body to die for, and a face that was more striking than a lot of women who were born to the role.

Michelle worked nights during our gay reviews. Occasionally, a portion of our straight day crowd would hang out for the evening show. One of my customers, a good-looking local wiseguy named Gus, was ogling Michelle every time she served him and his four buddies a round of drinks.

Finally, he called me over.

"Terri, who's the waitress?"

"Michelle."

"Is it okay if I buy her a drink? You know, have her sit down with us?"

Why not? I figured, keep the locals happy. I called her over and made the introductions. After twenty minutes, she was sitting on his lap, and he had his hands all over her. His friends were drooling. I felt it was my duty to inform Gus about Michelle's plumbing. I called him to the bar.

"You like her, Gus?"

"You bet," he said, a hungry leer in his eyes. "You mind if I leave with her?"

I put a sisterly hand on his shoulder and spun him around. "Gus, look around. You see what I have working here?"

He surveyed my help and shrugged. "Coupla fags, some broads."

"No, Gus. The transvestites, you pegged. The broads, as you put it, are transsexuals. Michelle, too."

He stared at me stupidly through drunken eyes. "Huh?"

"Jesus, Gus, she used to be a guy. She had the operation."

His jaw dropped. "You're fucking with me." Back at the table, Michelle was the center of attention. I just stared at him.

His brows knit, his lower lip stuck out. Gus was obviously thinking. "Fuck it, I still want to leave with her. She's fucking beautiful."

I tried to talk him out of it. Maybe Gus had some other issues, but who was I to stand in the way of true love? He was in heat.

They left together.

Gus came in the next day for lunch. To tell you the truth, I was surprised to see him. I figured that once he sobered up, he'd be too embarrassed to show his face. But he was all smiles. I cornered him at the bar.

"So, you take her to a motel?"

"Yeah."

"How was it?"

"Not bad. Wasn't as deep as it should've been, but not bad. She working tonight?"

＊　＊　＊

Business kept improving.

The joint was so popular that the first woman ever to escape from the Riker's Island jail did so for the express purpose of making the Friday night buffet.

"That fucking Terri can cook up a storm," she told her cellmates, who later ratted her out. "I'm getting the fuck outta here." She actually broke out of the jail, swam to shore, hailed a cab, and came to *Bill Bailey's*, after a short stop at a friend's house to change clothes. The cops were waiting for her as soon as she walked into the bar. Jail food will make you do strange things.

Good news and bad news: Nicki and I were rolling in money, but we rarely got a day off. We split the shifts to make certain that one of us was always in the bar, and it was beginning to take its toll. We needed a rest.

We hunted for a month until we found a reliable person to spell us while we took some time off. Jane Mackey, a thirtyish former bartender, came highly recommended by a friend of my father's who owned three bars.

"You'll never get anyone more honest and hard working than Jane. Smart, too."

Right on all counts. We hired her and sent spotters into the bar to see if she was stealing. She wasn't. We also tested her intelligence and stamina, giving her seemingly impossible tasks to accomplish to see if she would fold under the stress.

"Jane," I said, tossing her a set of keys over the

bar. "Go down to the storeroom where we keep the beer, and let me know how many seven-ounce glasses of beer we can get out of one keg. Allow for an inch-and-a-half of head."

Jane had a full bar. "C'mon, Terri, the place is jammed."

"Go, I'll watch the stick. You've got twenty minutes."

Dutifully, Jane went to the storeroom and began her count. She wasn't there a month before she became Jane the Brain.

Nicki and I agreed that we trusted her and that she was capable of running the business in our absence. Now we had to figure out where to go with our precious time off.

It was almost two in the morning, the crowd was thinning, and Nicki and I were at the bar putting away a bottle of Scotch.

"You got some place you want to go?" I asked.

"Not me, you?"

I shrugged. Great. We'd planned on at least a week off, and we had no destinations in minds. We killed the bottle talking up places we could go. Finally, after going through another half-bottle, I stood up, albeit unsteadily, and said, "Fuck it, let's leave."

Nicki looked at me through hooded lids. "Where to?"

"Miami. Tony's down there for another week." My husband was in Florida overseeing his hotel empire. He owned three hotels, at least that's what he told me.

"Good idea," Nicki slurred. "I gotta pack. You got an extra suitcase?"

"Sure." I grabbed two plastic garbage bags from behind the bar, handed her one. "Here you go."

And that's how we went to Florida. Two drunks with their worldly possessions jammed into garbage bags.

⁂

We stayed for a week. Tony was staying in a friend's hotel, under an assumed name ("checking up on the employees"). He got Nicki a room, and we partied for a week.

When we got back, Jane had everything under control. I retrieved my kids from my parents' house, and we were back to the old grind. A week later, Tony came home.

Business was never better, but it always seemed like we were chasing a dollar. True, we were accepting tabs, particularly from the wiseguys who were good for whatever they signed for, but it seemed like we should have been making a lot more money.

One afternoon, Nicki came into the bar three hours before her shift. She looked drawn.

"What's up?" I asked.

"We gotta talk."

We went to the office, and she made sure that the door was closed before she began. "I was at the bank today."

"We don't draw on Wednesdays," I said.

"I've got a savings account in the same bank."

"So?"

She licked her lips. "Tony was there."

"Yeah?"

"He didn't see me, but he looked around when he came in. I was with a manager in the back, talking about a car loan. I got suspicious, you know, the way he like, cased the place, like he was going to stick it up."

"Tony? What are you, nuts?"

"Maybe, but I asked the manager to check the

bar account after Tony left. He walked out counting a stack of bills."

I didn't like where this was going. Tony had been the closest thing to a model husband I'd had. Never a problem, good to the kids, always ready with a joke.

"Yeah?"

"He withdrew five large. Same thing for last week. Terri, Tony stole ten thousand from the business account."

"But he's not a signatory." I was in denial, subconsciously revisiting every bum I'd ever been involved with over the years.

"He forged the slip, Terri. Signed your name to it." Nicki couldn't look me in the eye.

We went through all the bank statements, really the first time we'd examined them closely. There were numerous unaccounted for withdrawals, although none as large as the two $5,000 transactions of the previous two weeks. Most were in the $200 to $600 range. The accountant that handled our books never said anything about the withdrawals, assuming that they were cash draws for Nicki and me.

I began a discreet background investigation on Tony. No need to hire a private investigator, the mob has tentacles all over the world. All it took was a few phone calls to our family's friends in Miami.

It wasn't long before I discovered the truth. Tony never owned any hotels. He was a professional gambler. He used the hotel story as a cover, not only to fool me, but everyone outside of his circle of gamblers and shylocks. For the first five months that we were together, he'd been on a lucky streak, followed by the inevitable losses. That's when he began tapping into the bar's account.

I confronted him, and he admitted what he'd done. He wasn't looking for forgiveness, and I wasn't looking to change yet another flawed man in my life. I asked him to leave, and he politely complied. We had been together for six months.

I felt like a failure, vowing this time not to get seriously involved with another man for the rest of my life, a promise I kept, for the most part, except for one serious romance that ended in disaster. I had no desire to ever marry again and was in no rush to divorce Tony (we wouldn't file for another ten years). After Tony, the only aisle I'd be walking down would be at the local supermarket.

❋ ❋ ❋

For a while, I wouldn't get beyond the talking stage with men. As soon as someone asked me out, I'd head for the nearest door. I realized after a few months that the head-in-the-sand attitude was ridiculous. I slowly came out of my shell and began dating again.

I did a complete one-eighty and went out with a detective from the Staten Island Task Force, a distinct departure from my usual type of man. His name was Joe DiNicola, a nice guy if there ever was one. Since I had no intention of getting move-in serious with the guy, he could have been a serial killer for all I knew, but on the surface, he was swell and treated me fine.

He knew my background, but didn't care. I made certain that he never met anyone from my family, and we both liked it that way. We were seeing each other for a few months when he began to get harassed by the Police Commissioner's Confidential Investigation Unit (PCCIU), the forerunner of the Internal Affairs Division. He was questioned about our relationship and followed wherever he went because it was assumed by the closed minds of the NYPD that he was seeing me because he was involved in some sort of criminal venture with my family.

At the same time, my partner, Nicki, began seeing a policewoman, a relationship that was kept confidential until Joe came under scrutiny. Nicki was renting an apartment in one of my father's apartment buildings. She and her lover were photographed leaving the building one night arm in arm. Not only was Joe's life being disrupted, but a ripple effect had been created, and other people were being affected.

Much to Joe's objections, I decided to break it off with him. I wasn't kidding myself; my family name was ruining his career and putting a lot of people under a microscope, my family included. Until John Gotti came along, wiseguys kept a low profile and wanted to keep it that way. We parted amicably and remain friends to this day.

With the business going well, it seemed like there was little in the wind to screw it up, but that was going to change.

❊　❊　❊

I've always had a bad temper. I never took it out on my kids or family, saving it for the poor schmuck, male or female, who might do or say something to piss me off. With my marriage a failure and Joe gone, I developed a very short fuse. Trouble looking to happen.

One day a local kid, he couldn't have been more than nineteen, came into the bar and began hustling pool games. Pool hustling is an art, and I congratulate anyone who has taken the time to learn the game and the patter to make a living behind a cue. This kid, while shooting a decent game, was also a thief and began taking advantage of my steady customers. He'd switch bills and palm money when his opponent wasn't looking, then have the balls to deny it when confronted. After he'd taken a few drunks to the cleaners, I stepped in.

"Give these guys their money back."

He sneered at me. "What the fuck for?"

"For stealing their money."

He got up in my face. At over six feet tall and husky, he was trying to intimidate a woman. This pissed me off. Without another word, I kicked him in the groin, and as he fell, I picked up his pool cue and parted his hair with it. He went down like a falling tree.

"Nicki," I called over my shoulder, "give me a hand with Fast Eddie here." We tossed him into the street.

For the next few days, I heard rumblings that he was looking to come back with a gun and take care of me. Then someone told him who I was. I certainly had my family name, but I also had a reputation for being a stand-up person and as such, got a lot of respect, all deserved. I ran a tight business, helped people who needed help, kept my mouth shut, and could be relied upon to do the right thing, reason for canonization in the world I knew.

About a week after the incident, the kid came into the bar with his hat in his hand, literally.

As soon as I saw him, I knew him he'd come to make amends.

"Miss Dee, remember me?" How could I forget him? In a darkened room I could identify him, by running my hands over the lumps on his head.

"Of course."

"Just came to apologize." He took a wad of bills from his pocket. "The dough I scammed from your customers."

I took the money. "Thanks. C'mon, have a drink."

He remained a good customer until I sold the bar.

❊　❊　❊

All stories don't have a happy ending. As I was closing the bar late one night, a uniformed police lieutenant and his driver, a patrolman, came in. It was after four o'clock, the legal closing time for bars in New York State. I had already cashed out, locked the register, and was waiting for the last of my customers to finish their drinks and leave. Just as long as I had poured their drinks before 4 AM, I was legal, so I really didn't think I had too much to worry about. The lieutenant had other ideas.

He was surly right from the start.

"You're running after hours."

"These drinks are backups, lieutenant, I'm cashed out, registers locked."

He glanced around while his driver walked around the room like he owned the place. Two more uniforms came in and stood at the door.

"This shit hole have a twenty-four-hour license?" the lieutenant asked.

I felt myself getting hot, but held my temper.

"We're not running a twenty-four-hour license. I told you these are backup drinks." My three remaining customers apparently didn't like where this was going and beat a hasty retreat without so much as a goodbye. "You want to see my license?"

The lieutenant looked me up and down at least twice.

"Yeah, get it, bitch."

That was all I needed. My one minute of restraint was history.

"Well, fuck you," I said and spit in his face. He lunged for me, but I had already stepped back. As he moved past me, I knocked off his hat and began pulling his hair. The three cops with him stood frozen for a split second, obviously not believing what they were seeing. When the lieutenant let out a howl, the cops sprung into action.

They pounced on me like I'd just fired a shot at the president. I went down under a pile of blue uniforms, but I bit and kicked with all I had. Before it was over, two more cops arrived, responding to a signal 10-13 (officer needs assistance), which is usually reserved for life-and-death situations. I was handcuffed and dragged kicking and screaming into a radio car. The porter had to close up that night; I was under arrest for assaulting six cops.

※　※　※

I was a bloody mess. My wrists were rubbed raw and bleeding from the cuffs being applied too tightly, and I had numerous cuts and contusions on my face. As bad as I looked, three out of the six cops looked worse. I had connected with a few good kicks to their faces. I was wearing boots that night and had inflicted maximum damage. One cop had a broken nose, the other a severely cut eyebrow that required stitches. The other cops had gotten away with bruised testicles and egos.

After being booked and tossed unceremoniously into a precinct holding pen, I flipped out on a policewoman who tried to enter the cell. I heaved my boots at her through the bars, narrowly missing her. Other prisoners weren't safe, either. I scratched the face of some poor woman who'd been locked up for intox driving because she asked me what I was in for. I didn't cool down for hours. The cops, I was convinced, had paid me that visit to shake me down for even more money than I was already doling out to half the cops in the precinct.

By the time morning came around, I looked like a wild woman: hair everywhere, clothes bloodied and torn. It looked like Alice Cooper had applied my makeup.

My lawyer, Paul LeMole, took one look at me and said, "Jesus, Terri, you can't go before a judge looking like that."

"Well, fuck you very much." I was in no mood to be nice, not even to Paul, who had represented the Dees for decades and was like a member of the family.

He called his office and had a woman come down with new clothes and shoes.

My father was notified. He must have called in every favor owed to him because the charges were dismissed at arraignment. I was free, but it wouldn't be the last time my temper got the better of me.

A few months later, I became the first woman in the history of the mob to be granted a sit-down with a Mafia capo because he had heard a rumor that I was gunning for his nephew. He was right.

❋ ❋ ❋

Respect. All my life I've been obsessed with it, preoccupied with earning it, and keeping it. My father and uncles had always stressed the importance of respect, that in our world being feared and respected was more important than being loved and revered. In order to survive, they needed people to know that when dealing with the Dees, they would get a firm but fair shake. Anyone that dealt honorably with my family could expect the same in return.

As a child, I saw the homage paid to my father and uncles wherever we went. They always got the best tables in restaurants, were sought after for their sage advice, and were generally treated like royalty. Such treatment came at a price. Toughness garnered respect, and my family was nothing if not tough. My family never forgot a slight, a gesture that meant disrespect. It might take years, but the Dees always got even. Cross my family and you'd have a problem.

It was with these values that I was raised, and it was these values that I lived by. So when the police paid me a visit and disrespected me and my business, I felt I had to retaliate, no matter what the consequences. While my family outwardly chastised me for getting arrested, I knew that they admired my spunk. Little Tiger was a stand-up person.

La Cosa Nostra is steeped in tradition. Women are considered second-class citizens and have no place in family business. We're put on this earth to have babies, cook, clean, and look good. We're expected to be on our husband's arms on Saturday evenings and to keep a respectful silence on Fridays, the mob's traditional Bimbo's Night Out. For me, this customary role for women wasn't an option. I conducted myself as my father and uncles did; cross me, show me any disrespect, and you paid the price.

✳ ✳ ✳

Friday night at *Bill Bailey's*. A virtual zoo. It seemed like every gay man and woman from the five boroughs was in the place. We'd exhausted ourselves by closing time, and I was looking forward to getting home and crawling into bed. Nicki was cleaning up behind the stick, the porter had just arrived, and the last remaining waitress, a transsexual named Maggie Hogan, was downstairs changing. We'd gotten rid of the last drunk an hour ago.

I was sorting out the credit card receipts when a knock at the door broke my concentration. A well-dressed guy of about forty waved me to the door.

"We're closed," I said through the glass.

"I'm Frankie Guzzio. I'm looking for the owner."

I knew the name, a wiseguy wannabe who liked to hang around with the made men. I opened the door.

"I'm the owner. What can I do for you?"

He looked at me quizzically. "No, the owner, Tony Dee."

"I'm Terri Dee. I'm the owner."

"I don't talk to no snatch. The owner, Tony DeLorenzo."

Wonderful. My estranged husband had passed himself off as the owner of *Bill Bailey's*.

"He's not here." I wasn't in the mood to explain my marital situation. I had let the "snatch" comment pass. The new me, tolerant with the assholes of the world.

He brushed past me, shoving me roughly aside.

"Hey!" I grabbed his shoulder. He pushed me away.

"Where's fucking Tony? He owes me money."

I got right up in his face. "Yeah, you and everybody else. I said he's not here. Now get out."

He gave me his best Richard Widmark sneer, must have practiced it in front of a mirror for hours. He looked around.

"This fucking place make any money?"

Nicki had come from behind the bar. "The boss told you to leave."

"Fuck you."

I heard a door shut to my left. Maggie Hogan must have heard the commotion and decided to come upstairs and investigate.

"Everything okay, Terri?"

Guzzio's eyes nearly popped out of his greaseball head. Maggie Hogan made Hulk Hogan look like Peter Pan. Before she became Maggie, she was Mike, a 220-pound dockworker. She'd slimmed down to a svelte 190, all of it silicone and muscle. She was wearing a leotard that could have doubled for a trampoline and a tight-fitting sweatshirt with a picture of Mick Jagger's tongue spread across her chest.

"What the fuck is that?" Guzzio said.

"This asshole giving you trouble, Terri?" Maggie said in her lilting tone. The woman made Broderick Crawford sound like Sir Laurence Olivier.

I was just plain tired of dealing with idiots. "Show dickhead the door, would you, Maggie?" Maggie Hogan had a fifth-degree black belt in karate.

Guzzio unbuttoned his jacket, slipped a hand into his pants pocket, and came out with a wicked-looking switchblade. It snapped open with authority. "Yeah, sure. You gotta be shittin' me. No fucking he-she is gonna–" Those were the last words he uttered.

Maggie was on Guzzio in a flash. The knife went flying, and she proceeded to wipe the floor with him. When last seen, he was airborne, sailing toward the gutter.

"Thanks, Maggie."

"Not a problem. Good workout."

But it was a problem. I went home that night and tossed and turned, unable to sleep. Guzzio had disrespected me, my help, and my bar. He had to be taught a lesson. He differed from the pool hustler who ran a scam on my customers. Guzzio was connected and should have done his homework before he came into my place of business and acted like an asshole. I saw no other alternative but to kill him. Overreaction? Not in my world.

⌖ ⌖ ⌖

It took me a few days to find someone who would sell me a gun and not inform on me to my father. During that time, instead of cooling down and forgetting the whole thing, I just got more and more pissed.

A local hood named Clem called and told me that he had an unregistered .25 automatic for sale.

"I'll take it."

"Don't you wanna know how much?"

"Not really." We agreed to meet in a restaurant on Mott Street in Manhattan that night.

Clem was at a table in the crowded restaurant, sipping a drink, when I arrived. He was in his twenties and bucking for his button, liked hanging around the social clubs and was willing to be a gofer to ingratiate himself with the bosses. He was the type of guy who could get any type of contraband or do the seemingly impossible at a moment's notice. Years later, he'd get into hot water for charging $5,000 to get screenplays from aspiring writers to Robert De Niro. The money went into his pocket, the screenplay into a shredder. The ultimate hustler.

I sat down, we exchanged pleasantries, and I ordered a drink. Clem passed the gun to me under the table. I slipped it into my purse.

"Three-fifty," he said. I counted out the bills and handed them over.

"It loaded?" I asked.

"I'm gonna hand you a loaded gun? What am I, crazy? Buy friggin' bullets. They're cheap."

My reputation had preceded me. I started to get up. He grabbed my arm.

"Stay, have dinner."

"Got an appointment, Clem," I lied. "Gotta run."

He maintained his grip. "I think we oughta talk."

"About what?"

"Word is you're gonna use that thing on Frank Guzzio."

I hadn't told a soul about what I was going to do, not even Nicki. "How'd you know?" No sense lying, I might find myself dead instead of Guzzio.

"I didn't. Jimmy Red did. Jimmy heard about the incident in your joint. Added two and two."

"You told him I was shopping for a piece?"

Clem shrugged. "Had to."

Jimmy Red was a captain in the Gambino family, a very powerful guy. He was an old-time mobster, about seventy and meaner than a junkyard dog. "Why does Jimmy Red give a shit about Guzzio?" I asked.

Clem bent over the table and lowered his voice. "Guzzio's a favorable witness in Red's son's trial next month. Nothing can happen to him. Guzzio testifies, Red's son walks."

I was in a spot. By all rights, once Jimmy Red found out that I wanted to clip Guzzio, I should have been history.

"Why am I still here?" I asked.

"Red wants a sit-down."

I was confused. "With who?"

"With you."

Even if the mob somehow became enlightened as to the role of women in modern society, Jimmy Red

140

would have been the last wiseguy illuminated. This old-time Mafioso wouldn't talk business with a female if his life depended on it. I smelled a rat.

"You've got to be kidding," I said.

"No joke, Terri. You've got a rep as a stand-up broad, and you got your family name. Red figures he owes you a sit-down, iron things out."

My heart was pounding like a piston. "Where am I supposed to go for this sit-down?"

"His bar on Spring Street."

"When?"

Clem looked at his watch. "About an hour. We got time to eat." He looked around for a waiter.

My head began to reel. The noise in the restaurant became strangely muffled as I grew warm and felt faint. I was wondering if Clem didn't give me rounds for the auto so I wouldn't be able to defend myself. I grabbed a glass of water and did my best to act nonchalant.

Was I having my last meal? I knew how these people operated. They'll break bread with you, then break your head, chop you up, and deposit you in the Staten Island landfill. But I had little choice but to stay and accept my fate. My sense of honor and respect for myself dictated that I face the music like a Dee. Getting up and walking out was out of the question. If I was wrong, if the meeting was legitimate, I'd look like a coward and lose the respect it had taken me years to acquire.

I had little appreciation for the fine cuisine. I picked and moved the food around my plate while Clem chowed down like he hadn't eaten in a week. Was he going to finally get to be a made man by whacking me?

The short ride to Spring Street was a blur. Clem pulled up in front of Red's bar and double-parked.

141

"You go in. Red's waiting." He smiled.

"You're not coming in?" My mouth was like cotton.

"Not my sit-down. I'll be here when you're through, take you to your car."

When I'm through.

"Yeah." I got out of the car on rubbery legs and walked toward my doom.

The door was locked. I knocked. Jimmy Red walked out of the darkness in the back of the bar and threw some locks. "C'mon in, Terri. I'm Red." He didn't offer a hand, but stepped aside and let me enter.

"Closed, huh, Red?" If I didn't sit down soon, I knew I was going to fall down.

"Mondays, you know. We get the Scarsdale mopes on weekends, the rest of the week sucks. I don't own this place to make money, you know what I mean?" Red was short and fat, with wisps of gray hair clinging to a shiny dome. This was a Mafia chief? He looked as threatening as George Burns.

It was well known that Red was worth millions, but you'd never know it to look at his clothes. He was wearing baggy corduroy pants and a flannel shirt stretched over his ample gut. He gestured to a table in the corner, then flipped on a wall switch. The room flooded with the comforting security of fluorescent light. We could be seen from the street through full-length windows. I felt a little better. Maybe I'd live after all.

"You want something? I got fresh espresso, a little sambucca?"

Yeah, I'm thinking, just give me the bottle of sambucca and a straw. "The espresso's good. Bring the bottle."

He vanished into the kitchen. This is it, I figured.

Clem comes through the door now and blows me away, then the cops come.

"You see anything, Jimmy?"

"Me? No. I was making coffee. Poor broad, they musta been after me."

Red came back after a few minutes. No Clem with a gun; nobody tossed a dead fish in my lap. We drank, made some small talk about our families, then he got down to business.

"Clem tell you about Guzzio?"

"Yeah."

"I need him for my kid. You want him dead, no?"

"He disrespected me, Red. I won't stand for that."

He sighed. "You're a stand-up broad, Terri, that's the only reason you're here. What can be done to make this right?"

"I don't know."

He thought a moment. "Whaddaya say I banish the fucking jerk from Staten Island? He can't come there no more. The whole fucking island, not just your place. Ever. That make you happy?"

It did. Guzzio never set foot on Staten Island again and was murdered fifteen years later, undoubtedly sentenced to death for his attitude. His killer was never caught.

Before I got back to my bar, word had spread that I was granted a sit-down with Jimmy Red. I was now a person to be reckoned with, someone to be treated with respect and definitely not to be trifled with. My life should have been smooth sailing from then on. I had a successful business, and my reputation would ensure that no one bothered me. But my cockiness and the heroin that was to later cloud my judgment would land me in the federal slammer.

9

Bucket of Blood

By 1976, *Bill Bailey's* was probably the most successful bar on Staten Island. We had people lining up seven nights a week to see our shows and gawk at the help. Since I had jettisoned Tony, Nicki and I were beginning to see some real money, and while the work was hard and the hours long, the rewards were worth it.

But in the bar business, along with crowds and increased notoriety, comes trouble. We were getting our share of fights in the place, and I was forced to hire a bouncer. Nicki and I could handle most any situation, but when brawls broke out among five men, we realized that we needed muscle.

I walked right into the clubhouse of the local chapter of the Breeds Motorcycle Club looking for the meanest, ugliest guy I could find who needed a few extra bucks and wasn't afraid to get his hair mussed. The Breeds made the Hell's Angels look like ladies who lunch.

Six men were sitting around a makeshift bar bullshitting, smoking dope, and drinking beer. My unannounced entrance startled them into silence.

Finally, a 400-pound refrigerator wearing a leather vest and no shirt said, "Fuck you want?"

"A bouncer." I told them who I was and what I owned. "A buck a night, off the books." A hundred dollars to these guys might not have been that much, considering the Breed was rumored to control all the crystal meth manufacturing on the Island, but bouncing meant that they could keep their pugilistic talents honed. If nothing else, these guys liked to rumble.

"That the fag joint?" a gorilla asked.

"That's the one. Anybody?"

They all wanted the job. I picked Tiny, the refrigerator.

❊ ❊ ❊

While Tiny controlled the door, it was up to Nicki and me to keep the natives on the inside manageable. Of course, Tiny was but a holler away, but I didn't want bloodshed inside the bar, if at all possible. I developed a system of dancing the unruly drunks out the door to avoid violence.

As soon as I spotted potential trouble, I'd grab the aggressor and ask him to dance. Sometimes I'd get a bum who didn't know his right foot from his left.

"But I don't dance," the drunk would say.

"Sure you do." I'd grab him around the waist and waltz him to the door where I'd hand him over to Tiny. "Toss Arthur Murray here, would you, Tiny?"

"You got it, boss."

My trouble would shortly be airborne into the gutter. The U.N. wouldn't have needed a peacekeeping force if it had Tiny and me.

Diplomacy didn't always work. For those occasions, I had a shotgun. I sawed six-inches off the barrel of an Ithaca pump and kept it behind the bar. I had maintained my youthful attraction to guns and wasn't afraid to use it. We had a bunch of street hookers who would try to get inside the bar to ply their trade, and more than once, I had to show them the door with the shotgun. These broads weren't shrinking violets; most carried knives and would cut you for looking at them wrong. A lesson learned from my Uncle Mike: Always bring a gun to a knife fight. I asked him once what he'd bring to a gunfight.

"A bigger gun."

I wasn't adverse to the girls plying their trade outside near the bar. My daytime customer base was mostly straight men. Show me a man who after six hours of steady drinking doesn't want to have sex. Or at least thinks he does. Their needs were mostly satisfied in the alley behind the bar. Live and let live was my attitude, until one day one of my best customers staggered into the bar after being gone for ten minutes and said, "I've been fucking robbed."

I came from behind the bar. "By who?"

He burped. "Carousel. She finished...you know, and when I picked up my pants my wallet was gone."

Carousel was a tough black prostitute, not altogether unattractive, with a reputation for being a bit bizarre. She had gotten her street name because she was once locked up for screwing a guy on a carousel. Not the amusement park ride, the luggage carousel at Kennedy Airport.

My customer Benny was a 60-year-old alcoholic retired telephone company employee with a face like a beat-up Chevy. He'd lost his wife to cancer and stood about as much chance at finding a decent woman and a normal sexual relationship as Hannibal Lecter. His outlet was hookers, the ten-dollar blowjob variety. My steady customers were like my family; I fed them, lent them money, and was invited to their homes for dinner (the ones that had homes).

Once again my "respect" jones kicked in. Mess with my customers, you mess with me. I grabbed the shotgun from behind the bar and made for the street. Nicki tried to stop me, but I shrugged her off. Tiny stepped in front of me at the door.

"Let me take care of this, Terri."

"My place, Tiny. Stand aside." Jesus, I sounded like John Wayne. I'd get back in touch with my feminine side later.

I spotted Carousel getting into her pimp's car near the corner. They stayed by the curb, engine idling. I sidled up to the passenger door, staying a little to the rear, so if she had a weapon, she would have to turn around to use it. I knocked on the door with the shotgun. Carousel turned white. I shoved the shotgun into the nape of her neck. She gasped.

Her pimp, Louie, a white guy I knew from the neighborhood, turned to me and threw up his hands. "Hey, Terri, put that fucking thing down."

"This little slut ripped off one of my customers, took his wallet in the alley."

"I didn't–" was all Carousel managed to get out before Louie backhanded her across the mouth with a hand laden with three heavy gold rings. Blood sprayed out the window, narrowly missing me.

Louie wasn't incensed that his whore had committed a crime, other than administering a blowjob in an alley for money, he was pissed that Carousel hadn't mentioned that she'd stolen the wallet. A portion of the proceeds were his.

She spit out a gob of red, and stammered, "I was gonna tell you, honey. I was–"

"Hey, shut the fuck up, and give Terri the john's wallet."

Carousel handed over the wallet. "Sorry."

"Louie, I don't want her working this block anymore, got it?" I poked Carousel in the head with the barrel of the shotgun for emphasis.

"Yeah, Terri, no problem. You got my word."

The word of a pimp. Not something you could take to the bank. But I never saw her again.

�֍ �֍ �֍

We had many other incidents in *Bill Bailey's*, some funny, some not. One time a deranged Middle Eastern cabdriver barged into the bar on a Friday night screaming "Ayatollah! Ayatollah," and brandishing a .45 automatic. He shot the place up pretty badly, but didn't hit anyone. Tiny took care of that one; he dragged the guy out the front door, never to be seen again.

One of my transvestite customers, a queen who called himself Ajax, got so drunk one night that I was afraid he'd kill himself or someone else if he got behind the wheel of a car. It was closing time, and I didn't want to babysit him all night, so Nicki and I led him to our office and deposited him on the couch. He was unconscious within seconds. We didn't want him getting to the booze, so we locked him inside and went home.

About two hours later, he woke up with a powerful thirst. He managed to slip the lock and make his way to the bar. In the process, he tripped the burglar alarm. The alarm sounded in three places: my house, Nicki's apartment, and the local precinct station house. Nicki, the cops, and I arrived at the bar at the same time.

The cops went in first, Nicki and I took up the

rear. The two young cops saw a light in the bathroom and barged in, only to find Ajax, dressed in a ballroom gown, peeing in the urinal with the gown hiked up around his waist.

The cops didn't know what to think. I said, "Ajax, put that thing away, and go back up to the office, you're drunk."

"Yes, dear," Ajax lisped, and stumbled out the door, but not before he tried to grab one of the cops' balls.

Stuff like this I don't think they teach in the Police Academy.

"Welcome to *Bill Bailey's*, officers," I said. "C'mon out front, we'll buy you a drink."

❀ ❀ ❀

My reputation as a stand-up person made me the target for people needing favors. Usually these favors came in the form of just released ex-cons looking for legitimate work. I had a soft spot for former felons looking to go straight, perhaps because of my lifelong exposure to men who had done time. Invariably, I'd either give them a job at the bar or find them something in the neighborhood.

One day, a tall, thirtyish, tough-looking Irishman came around looking for work. He introduced himself as Tommy Egan, said he'd just gotten out of the can where he'd done three years for robbery and needed work.

"I hear you're a stand-up broad."

"You're a real sweet talker. Can you handle a mop?"

We needed a porter at the time, and I hired him. Out of the many mistakes I've made in my life, hiring Tommy Egan has to rank up there as the worst.

Egan was one of the most intelligent people I'd

ever met. Extremely well read, he never went any-where without a book. He'd whip out a paperback waiting for a bucket to fill with water. He was up to date on international politics (very active in the IRA), economics, and read three newspapers daily, including the *Wall Street Journal*.

Egan was also one of the most violent men I've known, and I've known my share of violent men. He liked to hurt people. Egan was a true sociopath, with no conscience and an affinity for knives. He liked to get up close and personal when he damaged you, so guns wouldn't do.

I was smart enough not to get involved with him personally, but he was a fascinating person to talk to when he was sober, which wasn't often. He kept his brutal side away from the bar, at least at the begin-ning. Every so often, he'd attack one of the cus-tomers, but it was usually a drunk who was causing trouble. I'd gotten an extra bouncer in addition to a porter.

Egan could talk about the Irish Republican Army for hours. After a while, he talked me into attending a few meetings with him. Egan would get an empty envelope in the mail once a week. The return address was where that week's meeting was to be held. I'm not much for politics, but the fervor with which the people at the meetings spoke for their beliefs was inspiring. I contributed a few hundred dollars to the cause, but stayed in the background and watched the action.

✳ ✳ ✳

After a few months, Egan began to get more and more erratic. He'd get into fights in the bar con-stantly, stabbing people on several occasions. I fired him and barred him from the bar, but he'd manage to come in on a busy night and before I had a chance to throw him out, he'd beat or stab someone. It got to the point where we kept a mop and pail handy to clean up after Egan spilled some poor guy's blood. Needless to say, this guy was hurting our business. People were beginning to stay away.

I put the word out on the street that he'd have to deal with the wrath of the Dees should he ever show up in the bar again. The threat didn't faze Egan in the least. On more than one occasion, he was heard to say, "Fuck the Dees," and show up anyway, if just to stick his head in the door and either stab someone or hit some unfortunate guy over the head with a beer bottle. He began to carry a gun in a folded newspaper just in case he ran into one of my father's enforcers.

Eventually he was arrested for stabbing a customer in my men's room. The customer was good enough to tell the responding police officers that he'd gotten cut outside the bar, otherwise I might have lost my liquor license. Egan went to jail, and I figured I'd never see him again.

✳ ✳ ✳

After a while things got back to normal. The customers returned, and we were busier than ever. One afternoon as I was leaving my office, I tripped and fell down the entire flight of stairs that led to the bar on the floor below. I hurt my back seriously but refused to go to a hospital because I didn't want to leave the bar in the hands of the wait staff. Nicki wasn't scheduled to come in until that evening, and I couldn't track her down via phone. So I laid down on the floor in my office and suffered in silence.

The next day, I was in severe pain, so much so that my doctor had to make a house call. He recommended that I get to a hospital immediately, and an ambulance was dispatched.

After a series of x-rays, I was diagnosed with torn ligaments and tendons, plus major disc damage. An orthopedist recommended surgery, an opinion seconded by my personal physician.

I refused to consider an operation because I'd had friends who'd had back surgery and were in worse shape after the procedure. Plus, I was scared. I could go nose to nose with a rampaging wiseguy, but mention surgery, and I folded. I figured that given enough time, my back would heal itself.

Wrong.

※　※　※

Over the next few months, I got progressively worse. The pain was unbearable. Prescription pain medication had little or no effect. The thought of living in such intense pain made me think of suicide on more than one occasion. I lost my appetite, didn't care about my appearance as much, and generally looked like hell. The pain was etched on my face. But still, I made it to the bar every day and suffered through my shift, barely able to walk.

My savior, in the form of Tommy Egan, came strolling into the bar one morning when I'd just opened up and was alone. Egan would kick-start my trip into hell, from which I would not emerge for fifteen years.

I was alone in the back of the bar, taking a much-needed rest at a table when I saw Egan come in. He walked over, all smiles, like he had just seen me yesterday, when in fact he'd been in jail for his last stabbing. He looked fit, probably buffed from pumping iron, a con's therapy.

"Hey, Terri, how're you doing?"

I didn't–couldn't–get up. The thought of trying to throw him out never even entered my mind. I was incapable of lifting a glass of beer, let alone getting into a tussle with a man.

"You just get out?"

He smiled. "Two years, did it standing on my head." He snapped his fingers. Hoods always prided themselves on being able to do hard time without flinching. A badge of honor.

"Look, Tommy, I'm in no shape to argue with you. I'm just asking you to get out of my place, okay?"

He looked concerned, a trait I'd never seen in him before. Egan could gut-stab someone then go have a pizza. He liked to stab people in the stomach so he could hear the whoosh of air leaving his victim, like a deflating balloon. It would give him a rush. No, compassion wasn't high on Egan's list of character attributes.

"What's wrong? You look fucked up."

That just about summed up my medical condition. I told him about the fall, the pain, my inability to stop it. For some unexplained reason, talking about the accident and its aftermath made me feel better.

"I got a doctor could give you something to take care of that pain," he said.

I felt a glimmer of hope, but didn't want to believe that there was a doctor who could do something for me. I'd been to the best doctors in New York, and they had all recommended the surgery, with no guarantee of results. A few were honest enough to tell me I could wind up paralyzed.

"I've been to more doctors than I knew existed. No one can relieve this pain."

"I'm telling you, I got a guy. Give me fifty bucks, I'll go see him, get some medicine."

Logically I figured I was getting hit up for some spending money; give Egan the fifty and he'd go drink it up somewhere. But I wasn't thinking coherently; my pain was overriding my good sense.

I pointed to the bar. "The register's unlocked, I just put the bank in it for the bartender. Take fifty, do what you can do." I was grasping at straws.

He went behind the stick. "You won't be sorry." He opened the register and stuck bills in his pocket. "I'll be back in an hour."

After he left, I checked the register, certain he'd cleaned me out, but he'd only taken the fifty. I felt a surge of trust in Egan. Maybe he was on the level.

He was back in less than an hour. The day porter had come in, but the bar wouldn't be open for business for another half-hour. I was at the same table having coffee.

"Let's go to your office," Egan said.

We went upstairs, him leading the way. As I eased myself in the overstuffed chair behind my desk, Egan locked the door behind him.

"Roll up your sleeve," he said, as he removed a small metal box from his jacket pocket.

"What for?"

"Gotta give you an injection."

I've always been deathly afraid of needles, but after a little cajoling, he convinced me that the medication could only be administered via syringe. I was at the point where he could have stuck a turkey baster in my arm, I really didn't care.

With all my street smarts, I didn't know anything about drugs. I'd never touched a joint, much less smoked one. The cocaine boom was just gaining speed, but I had no desire to be an emaciated, sleep-deprived, nose-running zombie. Mind-altering drugs like LSD and peyote had never really scored big in

Italian neighborhoods. Heroin was considered so evil that the heads of the five families had a standing contract on any soldier who dealt in it.

So there I was, Terri Dee, Little Tiger: stand-up, street wise and tough, about to be shot up with a bag of smack, and I didn't know it.

❋ ❋ ❋

I was deathly ill. After Egan skin-popped the dime bag of heroin into my arm, I immediately began sweating and throwing up.

"Jesus, Tommy," I complained, "I'm dying." I was writhing on the floor, convinced that I was going to die. "What was that shit?"

Egan shook his head. "It happens the first time you take it. Strong medicine. Next time it'll be better."

I folded into the fetal position. "There's not going to be a next time."

"Your pain's gone, no?"

I was too busy barfing in the trashcan by my desk to notice. Egan was right. No more pain. I was cured.

Once a day, every day for the next three months, Egan would shoot me full of dope. I still had an aversion to needles, so Egan had to do the honors. I was blissfully unaware of what I was taking. All I knew was that the pain was gone and that I felt the best I'd felt in years.

At the end of three months, I'd graduated to two-dime bags a day. To my way of thinking, twenty dollars a day was a small price to pay for the feeling of euphoria and the pain-free days Egan's "medicine" provided.

Egan was once again a fixture in the bar. He was getting into fights again, but I was hesitant to have him thrown out because he was supplying me with my daily double shot. Nicki began to get angry with me, but I didn't care. I was on another planet. No one knew I was taking anything, let alone heroin. Egan wanted his role in curing my pain kept between the two of us. I was a functioning junkie, able to work and provide for my kids.

About five months into my addiction, Egan stabbed the wrong guy and got locked up again. While he was in jail awaiting release on bond, I began to have withdrawal symptoms. I thought I was going to die and didn't know why I felt that way. I thought I was getting the mother of all viruses. I can only equate the feeling with being seasick, only a hundred times worse. Still, I hid my battle with withdrawal from Nicki, the help, and my family. It was pure hell, but I persevered until Egan got out, and the cycle began all over again.

❋　❋　❋

Tommy Egan was making enemies all over Staten Island. A lawyer with IRA sympathies had charged him $3,200 to defend him in the last stabbing case. When the complainant got cold feet and withdrew his complaint, Egan demanded his money back. When the lawyer told him he'd earned his fee, Egan pulled a knife on him. He got his money back, but the head of the Staten Island faction of the IRA, who had personally recommended the lawyer, was quite put off by Tommy Egan and banned him from the organization.

Egan also liked to go to bars, order drinks until he was stupefyingly drunk, and then refuse to pay his tab. He'd just tell the bartender to go fuck himself and walk out. If anyone tried to stop him, they'd get ventilated with a blade.

Tommy Egan found himself in the position of being hated by almost every tough guy on Staten Island, not an enviable position to be in. He managed to get himself locked up for some minor offense just to get off the street and out of harm's way. By the time he got out, he figured, all the animosity would be forgotten, and he could get back to his old ways.

In the meantime, I was in serious trouble. I desperately needed my twice-a-day fix or I couldn't make it out of bed. I called Egan's friend, Sal. He came over the house after the kids went to school. I figured he would know Egan's "doctor" friend.

He took one look at me and knew I was a junkie. I pleaded with him to get me my "medicine."

"Look, kid," Sal said, "I'm not going to lie to you. Tommy's been giving you heroin."

Initially, the revelation didn't register. But after a few minutes, when I realized that the symptoms I'd been experiencing were from my body craving more dope, I came to understand that Tommy Egan had purposely gotten me hooked. He was my personal pusher.

I felt immediate rage, my murderous fury overriding even my need for more heroin. Shortly, however, I knew that I needed another shot, if only to clear my head and figure out how I was going to get the monkey off my back.

Sal became my supplier as I degenerated slowly into heroin hell. The next shot was all I lived for. My business began to suffer. Nicki demanded that I sell out to her. I complied. I wanted more money for junk. My house was next. With no business and no means of support, I defaulted on my mortgage payments, and the house was taken by the bank.

Still, like every junkie since time began, I hid my

addiction. I told my parents that I had sold the house. I functioned as a mother, went to PTA meetings, cooked, and cleaned, but I lived for the next boost.

I still couldn't stomach the thought of sticking a needle in my arm, so Sal shot me up. When he wasn't around, I'd score in the East Village in Manhattan. A black junkie who called himself Cleveland mainlined me. He charged me four dollars for his services.

❃ ❃ ❃

After Egan was released from jail, and before I'd sold out to Nicki, he heard that I found out that he'd been shooting me full of heroin. He stopped into the bar to talk me into using him again as my connection. No more pretense; he was just another pusher looking for a customer.

He showed up on a Friday night. Tiny waylaid him at the door and had a customer find me.

I went blind with rage when I saw him, and Tiny had to keep the two of us apart.

"Get the fuck out of my bar!" I screamed. The room went deathly silent as the show stopped and all the customers gaped at me.

Egan smirked. "Yeah, sure, Sugar," and as he turned to leave, he grabbed a full beer bottle from a window ledge and slammed it over a customer's head. The poor guy had walked in the door at exactly the wrong time. His head gushed blood immediately. Tiny made a grab for Egan, but he slipped his hold and ran down the block.

The next day, I heard that Egan had gone to another bar after he'd left my place, ran up a tab, and refused to pay. He'd been jumped by three guys and seriously beaten. Three weeks later, he was back on the street doing the same things: beating and stabbing total strangers and stiffing bartenders. He didn't, however, come back to *Bill Bailey's*. It was just a matter of time, I knew, before someone would dispatch him. As far as I was concerned, it couldn't happen soon enough.

❋ ❋ ❋

My wish came true three weeks later. Egan, while climbing the stairs to his rooming house, was shot in the back of the head. His killer escaped.

I got the call from one of the first cops on the scene. I'd put the word out to the precinct cops to let me know when Egan got his just reward. A hundred dollars went with the notification.

"Terri," the cop said and identified himself. "Your boy just got clipped."

I was having a rough day. Sal was late, and I was debating going to Alphabet City in the East Village to score. I was up to four bags a day.

"Where?"

"Front of his shit-hole apartment. Guy jumped out and put one in his head. Never knew what hit him. Shooter got away."

"You sure it's Egan?" I was talking through my pain.

"Of course I'm sure. Body's still here. Come down see for yourself."

"I'll be right there." I had to see firsthand that the person who had put me through this hell was actually dead. I needed it for closure before I went for the cure, something I'd promised myself I'd do. Right after the next shot.

"Bring a hat, it's getting cold," the cop said.

"Hat" was cop speak for money. I owed him the hundred. I knew all the police terminology after

Already a budding ice
queen at age seven.

With my brother John
when I was five years old.

In my dream home
with Tommy Ernst.

Cutting the wedding cake with Frank Aron, husband number one (October, 1956).

Anthony Buttino, husband number two and brother-in-law of Vincent "Chin" Gigante.

With Anthony Buttino and our son, John.
The twins are from my first marriage.

With "sportsman" Anthony
DeLorenzo, husband number three
and still a good friend to this day.

Me at age thirty-five.

Relaxing in Palm Beach. I'm the one seated on the left.

On the set of *The Godfather* film with Gianni Russo, the actor who played Carlo, the wife-beating husband of Talia Shire. I'm standing on the far right.

At a 1974 party in Cherry Grove, Fire Island. All of the individuals in the photo are gay, except for me.

Practicing karate with Nicki, the co-owner of our bar.

Debra, our beautiful transvestite wait-person who attracted male patrons.

Sweetie, a popular transvestite.

My identification card at the
Metropolitan Correctional Center, 198

An attractive transvestite
performing in a drag show
at the bar in 1973.

With my son John, a Navy
SEAL, in 1988. He died of a
heart attack four months after
this photo was taken.

With my brothers, Pat and Johnny, in 1968.

With my twin sons, Ronnie (on left) and Frankie (on right).
They are now forty-three years old.

My father with my newly discovered daughter.

Me today.

years of feeding and bribing them. I giggled stupidly. I was trilingual: English, cop, and wiseguy. When
I cleaned up, I could get a job at Berlitz. Right after
the next shot.

❋ ❋ ❋

A body covered with a bloodstained sheet was
sprawled halfway down a flight of weather-beaten
wooden stairs. The cop who had called me led me
under the yellow POLICE–DO NOT CROSS crime
scene tape after I slipped him his cash.

I was shaking as I neared the body, not from
fright or anger, but because I was still overdue for
my noon shot.

"Could you take the sheet away? I want to see
him."

"Sure."

The cop lifted the sheet far enough for me to see
the face. Despite a rather nasty exit wound, Egan
was recognizable. I stared at him for a few seconds.

The cop standing next to me was a little jumpy.
"You shouldn't really be here, Terri. A boss comes,
I'm fucked."

I barely heard him. As the cop gently grasped my
arm, I shrugged him off and began to kick the life-
less pusher who had ruined my life.

"Sonofabitch! You worthless motherfucker!"
Tears streamed down my face as the cop tried to
restrain me. I wasn't about to leave until I either
collapsed or was arrested.

It took three cops to pull me away from Egan's
body. I was in no shape to drive myself home. The
officer who had called me got me a cab, gave the driver some bills to take me home. He could afford it.

❋ ❋ ❋

I was a strung-out, broke junkie, with no prospects

for the future. I'd been living off savings and the rest of the money that Tommy Ernst had stashed before he was murdered. My parents didn't know that I'd sold my interest in the bar. The money was just about gone, most of it spent on heroin. I needed cash, and I needed it quickly.

Shortly, I would become a full-time criminal, complete with my own gang and more money than I could ever hope to make legitimately. I would also wind up in jail, convicted on a variety of federal crimes. Worth it? Of course not, but the thrill of making the money and calling the shots in a criminal enterprise was a high unto itself. The consequences, however, are nearly always inevitable.

10 Wall Street Scam

By 1981, three years after I'd become hooked on drugs, I was desperate for money. While I had maneuvered myself into managing two Staten Island bars, I was putting my salary in my veins. My reputation as a good businesswoman had preceded me, and I had no trouble obtaining the managerial positions. But I was after *real* money, an amount that could support me, my family, and my habit in the manner to which I had become accustomed.

I figured I had two choices: sponge off my family or do something crooked. I was leaning toward the latter. Then two things happened during the summer that would propel me in that direction.

One sunny afternoon when I should have either been working or spending time with my family, I was in Alphabet City scoring dope. After Cleveland shot me up, I took the ferry home and was confronted by my twins, Ronnie and Frank, at the door. Both were visibly shaken.

My heart sunk. "What happened?" My first thought was that a member of my family had been killed.

"Two guys, Ma, come around a little while ago looking for Tony," Ronnie said. "We told him you weren't married to him anymore, and he didn't live here. They didn't believe me."

"Yeah," Frank said. "Then they said Tony owed them money, and they were going to burn the house down unless he paid it."

My boys were literally shaking. Both boys were in college, not children by any means, but I had shielded them from the life, as my parents had tried to do. They hadn't known any of the violence or intimidation associated with it. I was livid beyond description, but held my temper.

"What'd they look like?"

They described two lowlifes named Wigs and Larry, buddies of my estranged husband. After I calmed them down, I began making phone calls. Within minutes, I got the whole story.

Wigs and Larry had given Tony a stack of stolen "B" bonds to fence for them. The closest Tony had ever come to a fence was when he bumped a lawn-mower against the wooden one in our yard. Tony was a gambler. Stolen property wasn't his forte. He must have been broke, promised Wigs and Larry a good return, and supplied his old address in case they needed to get in touch, after which he absconded with the bonds.

I went to *Bill Bailey's*. Even though I sold out to Nicki, we still maintained a good relationship. She was, however, surprised to see me. I breezed into the bar and went behind the stick for the shotgun.

"Oh oh," Nicki said.

I told her the story.

"Let me get Tiny, Terri. He'll talk to them."

"These are my kids, Nicki. No one threatens my

family. What happens if they come back and torch my house?"

She thought about that. "Be careful."

Wigs and Larry hung out in a bar in Brooklyn called the 19th Hole, a notorious mob hangout. I stuck the shotgun in a shopping bag and called for a cab.

✳ ✳ ✳

"Circle the block," I told the driver.

The bar was located on a residential street in Bensonhurst. I was checking to see if the place was under police scrutiny, the main reason I'd left my car at home. I didn't spot the usual unmarked black van with tinted windows that even Stevie Wonder could make for a surveillance vehicle. I told the driver to let me off at the other end of the block.

I was hit with a blast of cold air conditioning as I entered the darkened bar. After my eyes adjusted to the dim lighting, I saw a group of six men in T-shirts at a table in the back playing cards and drinking espresso. The game came to a halt when they saw me.

"Closed, lady," a fat guy said. "We open at six."

"Then you should lock the door." I whipped out the shotgun, let the bag fall to the floor, and walked toward them.

Chairs scraped, hands went up.

"Hey, lady!" a skinny guy with a bad rug said.

"Where're Wigs and Larry?" I leveled the shotgun at them.

An older man with a cigar hanging limply from his lips said, "She's flyin'."

I was fresh off a shot. The pupils of my eyes must have looked like two pinholes in the snow. "You're goddamn right I'm high. Now where's those two guys?" I swept the shotgun across the table. No one moved.

"Hey, let's talk about this, lady. They ain't here," a young guy said.

It took them a good ten minutes to calm me down. After they found out who I was (and gently removed the shotgun from my sweaty hands), the old guy with the cigar, who seemed like he was the boss, sat me down while the rest of his crew left the bar. Probably to change their underwear.

I told him the story. "They threatened my kids. Tony's my *estranged* husband. They want to find him, tell them to try Florida."

"These guys, they're a little fucking crazy, but I'll talk to them. You gotta promise no more shotgun shit."

I promised. We had a drink. It was over. For now.

❋ ❋ ❋

I was jumpy enough from the heroin (or usually, lack of it), but now I was even more paranoid. I hadn't heard a thing in three weeks. I'd expected either some kind of a truce offering from Wigs and Larry or an attempt on my life. What should have been a reasonable resolution to our problems after my conversation with the boss in the 19th Hole could go the other way because I was a woman. No self-respecting wiseguy liked to be dissed by a female. I could see an ambush coming, Dee or no Dee.

I was accessorized by the shotgun, went nowhere without it. When I stopped at a red light, I'd make sure that I had enough room between my car and the car in front of me to be able to make a hasty getaway if I had to.

Finally, during the fourth week, I was sitting in my living room watching TV with one eye and the street with the other when I spotted a dark blue Buick cruise the block and slowed in front of my house.

Wigs and Larry were in it.

I grabbed the shotgun from beneath the sofa cushions, went to the front door, and waited. I had just shot up and was feeling no pain.

The Buick came back and stopped in front of the house.

I burst through the screen door like a crazy woman and ran for the car, screaming obscenities all the way. Wigs, who was in the passenger seat, threw his arms in the air.

"Floor it, Larry, she's a fucking psycho!"

The car peeled away in a haze of burnt rubber and acrid smoke.

I fired a shot in the general direction of the car, never bothering to aim.

"Yeah, I'm a fucking psycho!" I screamed. "You come back here and you'll see how much of a psycho I am!" I cycled another round and fired a second shot into the air. The Buick disappeared around the corner.

I mumbled to myself as I made my way toward the house. My next-door neighbor, a nosy old man, came out onto his porch. "What's going on?"

I pointed the shotgun at him, and he took off back inside his house. "Mind your own goddamn business!"

Little Tiger, totally in control.

The following day I got a call from the old gangster who had counseled me in the 19th Hole in Brooklyn.

"They were coming to apologize, Terri."

I couldn't believe it. "So why'd they circle the block? Why didn't they just come up to the house? "

"Couldn't find a place to park."

I thought about it. He was right; there were no parking spots anywhere near my house yesterday.

So now, in addition to having a reputation as a stand-up person, I was also known as a fearless lunatic.

❋ ❋ ❋

I'd show up for work when I felt like it, which wasn't too often, telling the two old men who owned the bars that staying away was part of my managerial strategy. I called it long-distance supervision. That excuse would get me another three weeks of employment until the staff robbed the place blind in my absence.

The drugs had made me too lazy and strung out even to go food shopping. My money was rapidly dwindling, and I was running a tab at the local supermarket. A kid named Ralphie delivered my groceries twice a week.

A nice boy, around seventeen, he would sometimes stick around for a few minutes for a soda on a hot day. My kids liked him, too.

One day, he looked like he'd lost his best friend, face down to his shoes.

"What's wrong with you?" I asked.

At first he was reluctant to say anything, but finally he opened up. He had taken a loan out on the street, three hundred from a shylock.

"I been paying the thing off for two years, Terri, musta paid four times what I borrowed. The guy won't let me alone. Six points a week in vig. It's never gonna end."

"You're a bright kid," I said, "you could do the math."

"That was then, this is now. I need tuition money for school, I start Baruch in three weeks."

I got the name of his shylock out of him, but Ralphie wouldn't hear of me going to talk to the guy. He'd pay off his obligation *and* handle school, no matter how long it took. Another Italian with a hard head.

After swearing that I wouldn't interfere, and after Ralphie left, I called my father and asked him to set up a meeting with the shylock for me.

"You wouldn't be looking for a loan, would you, Tiger?"

"Who me? I'm loaded."

❊ ❊ ❊

We met in *Bill Bailey's*. The shylock was a retired NYPD captain who'd hooked up with the Gambinos when he left the job. He began as a bookmaker, expanding to putting loans out on the street with his extra cash. He answered to my Uncle Pope and was eventually murdered in 1989. Must have lent money to the wrong person.

"Pope knows nothing about this," I said. "I'm asking a personal favor. Let the kid off the hook. Enough's enough."

He thought about it for a while, apparently trying to make the right business decision. "Okay," he said. "Goodwill, you know?"

❊ ❊ ❊

Ralphie stopped by to thank me.

"I thought I asked you not to get involved," he said.

"You're a good kid," I said. "You don't need a hosing. Go to college, get a decent job. Or maybe you'd like to continue paying the vig for the rest of your natural life?"

He laughed. "Listen, Terri, I got a friend of mine, maybe latched onto something he can't handle by himself. Thought you might be interested. Takes some balls, but you got them. Everybody heard about what happened in the 19th Hole."

Ralphie, like every neighborhood kid, knew exactly what was going on in the community. I'd helped him out of a jam, now it was payback time. Whatever he'd heard about, I knew that it wasn't legal, but I was in dire financial straits and was willing to listen to anything.

"Who's your friend?" I asked.

"Jimmy Collins."

Jimmy Collins was a local burglar who liked to hang out with Italian gangsters. I knew him from the neighborhood. He had a good reputation, kept his mouth shut, and gave tribute to the local bosses whenever he made a big score on a burglary.

"Send him around." I said, unknowingly sealing my doom.

❀ ❀ ❀

"I think I got something big, Terri, but I need connections to get it done," Collins said. He was nervous, fidgeting, and chain-smoking. A slight guy, he couldn't have weighed more than me. I figured that any second he'd launch himself into orbit.

We were sitting in my living room on a Monday night. The kids were asleep.

I was on my second Scotch on top of a dime bag, feeling no pain. "I'm listening."

"You know Wall Street at all?"

"I know it's a train stop away from Little Italy. Other than that, I don't invest. All my money's tied up in cash."

He leaned closer, conspiratorially, even though we were the only people in the room.

"I'm going down there like once, twice a week to

pick up my girl. She works for some stockbroker. So I'm in the lobby of this big building waiting, you know, and I see this friggin' mailbag there every day.

"So one day, I lift the friggin' thing. Just throw the bag over my shoulder and bring it to my car. I go through it. You know what's inside?"

"Mail?" I was bored, feeling mellow, and not very interested.

"Yeah, some of that, but other stuff, too. Checks, Terri. Like fifteen, twenty of them."

Now I was interested. "How much?"

He shrugged. "About half of them, no big deal. In the hundreds. But the other half," he shook his hand, "like twenty, thirty large, all made out to individuals. Dividend checks."

Ka-ching! Ka-ching! A cash register was playing a tune in my head. We steal that bag, cash the checks, we're rolling in money.

Collins saw the dollar signs in my eyes. "But that ain't all. I took a walk around the neighborhood. Most *all* the goddamn buildings have the same thing, mailbags in the lobbies." He began to giggle like a school kid.

We put our heads together. Jimmy Collins, my new best friend, needed a way to cash the checks before they were reported stolen. This is where he figured my connections would come in.

"We're gonna need ID," I said. "I know a guy can phony up a driver's license and voter's card in a few minutes." New York State was one of the last states to require photos on driver's licenses, and that change was still two years away.

We talked for hours. It was agreed that I would run the operation, and I suggested that we get another four people involved. Even split.

"We grab the mailbags, take them to our car, sift through them for the checks, then return the bags."

"Why a six-way split?" Collins asked.

"After we get the checks, I call my ID connection, tell him what we need. I pick up the ID the next day, we sign the checks and fan out all over the city to cash them. The more people involved, the faster we can cash the checks before they're reported stolen."

Collins thought I was a genius. God knows how much more sophisticated I could have made the plan if I'd have been straight.

※ ※ ※

I arranged for the crew: four local wiseguys I'd known most of my life and felt that I could trust. The deal with the forger was $50 per forged document, a steal (pardon the pun), considering how much money we figured to score.

We did two dry runs, five of us in one car, Collins in another. My car would contain the "boosters," the actual thieves. Collins would drive the "sorting car," where the checks would be separated from the rest of the mail. I'd drop the boosters at four buildings, circle around, and begin retrieving them. By the time I dropped off the last booster, or so the theory went, the first one would already be separating the checks in Collins's car.

I brought a stopwatch. We went through the motions, not stealing anything, not even touching the mailbags. It was all pantomime. Marcel Marceu would have been proud.

Everything went smoothly. We were ready to seek our fortune.

※ ※ ※

Despite being fueled by heroin and a lust for money, I was less nervous than I thought I'd be. I gathered my crew at a local Staten Island diner and took off for Manhattan's financial district.

I began dropping off the boosters at 2 PM. Within forty minutes, we had checks totaling over $32,000. Bingo!

After we discarded the few checks made out to women, I drove to Brooklyn, made my call to the forger, giving him the names I needed IDs for.

"That's a lot of paper, Terri," he complained. "Gonna take a while."

"Take your time. How's tomorrow, say nine in the morning sound?"

"I was talking four or five hours. You can stop by tonight, you want."

The banks didn't open until 9 AM. I didn't need a rush job, but he had no idea why I needed the ID. This was "need to know," and he didn't need to know. "Tomorrow's good."

The crew and I assembled at my house for the check-signing ceremony. I made the drinks while my guys signed. This became a ritual; when we got to my place, I'd break out the booze, maybe cook something, while everyone else signed checks. When we eventually got busted, my role as cook and bartender would save me from a longer prison sentence. But I'm getting ahead of myself.

❋ ❋ ❋

The next day was the acid test. I picked up the ID before I picked up my crew: another "need to know" rationale. Why jeopardize the forger? Who knew when he might come in handy again. After we assembled, we drove to Manhattan and started hitting banks. Occasionally I'd go into a bank with a check casher, reasoning that if we somehow got a suspicious banker, I'd create a diversion while my guy made a getaway. Staying a distance away from my man, I was prepared to hit the floor and throw a fit.

I also made the decision to have the check casher go directly to a bank officer, rather than a teller, for check approval. These checks were in the $5,000 range, and I knew that tellers would require bank officers to sign off on them if we didn't have an account in the bank. Why create a situation where my check casher would stand out by having to leave the teller's line and return after he got the check approved by a bank officer? The lower the profile, the better the chance for success.

Everything went smoothly. Because none of the checks were made out to people who held accounts at the particular bank, the bank officers invariably asked for ID. They'd peruse the phony paperwork and initial the checks.

❋ ❋ ❋

We were on a two-day-a-week schedule for the first three weeks. Then, realizing how easily we were getting away with the scam, we increased the thefts to every business day. After surveying numerous office buildings in the area, we determined that practically all of them left mailbags in the lobby. Therefore, we never ripped off the same building more than three or four times a month. My share was about $6,000 a day.

I was in heroin heaven, all my bills were paid, and my family and I were living the good life. The operation could go on almost indefinitely. I knew how cops worked, or rather how they didn't work. They weren't very efficient and certainly not computerized in the early 1980s.

Reports of lost checks had to be making their way to the police after the first week or two of the scam. After three or four weeks, the cops would know that the checks were being cashed, which would mean that they were stolen, not lost. They would assume that the checks were being ripped off from individual mailboxes, a common crime in those days, and not from the brokerage houses themselves.

The New York City Police Department was highly compartmentalized back then. A perfect example of this would be the Son of Sam murders a few years before. Three murders were committed before the NYPD realized that it had a serial killer on its hands, despite the same weapon being used in all the shootings. This was because the killings occurred in different precincts, and one hand didn't know what the other was doing. It finally took Jimmy Breslin, a reporter from the *Daily News*, to connect the crimes.

Reports of the stolen checks would be filed in individual precincts and not shared with other precincts or a centralized command. This was the crack-fueled 80s; people were getting murdered by the thousands in the five boroughs. Who gave a damn about a bunch of stolen checks? To the NYPD's way of thinking, an arrest would be made when someone was caught in the act of cashing a stolen check. And that wasn't about to happen to any of my crew. We were too well papered up with phony ID to be concerned.

We did have one close call. A bank manager didn't take one of the phony driver's licenses at face value and decided to call the issuing brokerage.

My man was in the bank manager's office on the second floor, the only means of escape being down the elevator or down a flight of stairs at the end of the hall. Either way, if he had to run, it would take him more than enough time for the bank manager to either hit an alarm or call one of the guards on the first floor.

When I saw my guy go into the elevator, I went up the stairs and loitered around the manager's door. I heard him tell my check casher that he was going to call the brokerage and planned a blocking maneuver should there be a foot chase. Fortunately, the brokerage gave a green light for the check, it hadn't as yet been reported stolen.

❀ ❀ ❀

We were into our fifth month of stealing checks, and everything was still going smoothly when, unbeknownst to the rest of us, Jimmy Collins got arrested for burglary and decided to inform on my crew. He sang like the proverbial bird and worked out a sweet arrangement where he wouldn't be charged with either crime if he could deliver us to the police.

What started like another day at the office began with our usual meet in the diner's parking lot. Everything seemed normal. We proceeded to Manhattan in the two cars, ready to make another big score.

As usual, things went smoothly. We got back to Staten Island before the rush hour. The crew in my car was sedate, the thrill of stealing the checks had worn down to a mundane daily commitment. I pulled into the diner's parking lot first, Collins right behind me. We would use our individual cars to get to my house for the signing of the checks.

As I got out of the car, I turned for a split second. I saw Collins get out of his car and run a hand through his hair. Instinct kicked in. I knew, just from that casual movement, that we'd been set up. Adrenaline coursed through me; I was in fight or flight mode, looking around for a means of escape.

Too late.

Within seconds, six unmarked cars zoomed into the street, and cops jumped out, guns drawn.

We were busted.

We were handcuffed and separated, one prisoner per car. The caravan lined up and headed for the nearest police precinct.

I had to think quickly and try to extricate myself from the situation.

"Excuse me, Detective?" I squeaked from the backseat.

My arresting officer was a burly Irishman who hadn't said anything to me after reading me my rights.

"Yeah?"

"I think we should talk."

"What, the cuffs too tight?"

"The cuffs are fine. My name's Dee, you know my family?" I saw him look at me in the rearview mirror.

"Yeah, I know them. Which one are you?"

"Terri. John's my father. Could we talk about this?"

He was quiet for a few moments. The convoy of cars glided through the quiet residential streets of a peaceful Staten Island on a cold winter's day.

"You got any pictures of your family in your wallet?"

"Yeah. You have my purse."

He kept one hand on the wheel and rummaged through my bag with the other. After coming up with my wallet, he thumbed through the pictures.

"Your Uncle Pope and your father in this one, huh?" He held it up.

"Yeah." I looked for a street sign. We were three

blocks away from Pope's wire room. "We could go talk to Pope."

The detective picked up the radio and said, "Gotta make a pit stop, see you at the house." He turned right at the next street. He knew exactly where he was going.

❊ ❊ ❊

It cost my Uncle Pope $1,500 to buy my freedom. But there was a major caveat.

"If the feds pick up on this, our deal is off," the detective said as he stuffed the money into his pocket.

"I understand," Uncle Pope said. The brokerages were insured by the FDIC, and if the FBI became aware of the case, they'd take it over. It was also agreed that I'd still go to the station house in cuffs, be segregated from the men, and eventually be cut loose. "Lemme talk to the kid for a second, Detective, before you two go, okay?"

The cop shrugged. "Yeah, sure."

Uncle Pope led me rather roughly into another room.

"What the fuck're you doing? Your father'll shit."

I wasn't interested in a morals lecture. "What I'm doing is thirty large a week."

His eyebrows shot up. "Each?"

"Each."

End of lecture. My uncle understood a good score. He wouldn't have passed up the chance at that kind of money, either.

He hugged me. "Good luck. Looks like you're home free."

Not quite.

❊ ❊ ❊

The booking process at the station house was a

sham, at least as far as I was concerned. I was kept segregated from the men, as is NYPD policy, but while they were in a cage on the second floor, I was in the captain's office downstairs making coffee.

I watched as my crew was led away from the station house in chains on the way to criminal court for arraignment. Oddly missing was Jimmy Collins. What a surprise.

I was home in time for Johnny Carson. I'd managed to sock away a large portion of the money I'd stolen. While I was still a hard-core heroin user, anyone who could pour those kinds of profits into their arm would be dead. I was going to be financially stable for the foreseeable future.

❀ ❀ ❀

Things went well for the next six months. My crew was out on bail, and no one begrudged me my ability to bribe my way out of an arrest. What they did want to do was get their hands on Jimmy Collins, who hadn't been seen in the neighborhood since the bust. If he was smart, he'd have left the country. It appeared as if, with plea bargaining, the crew would get off fairly light. None expected to do more than a year in jail. Considering the money they'd made, no one had a gripe.

I'd been seriously trying to quit the drugs. My family and most of my friends were still in the dark. I still functioned as if I were straight, but my habit was up to five bags a day. I knew that if I kept it up, I'd eventually overdose or be arrested when I made a buy. I owed it to my children and myself to get clean.

My efforts to kick the habit amounted to no more than trying to go cold turkey on at least five occasions. Addicts who can successfully clean up by abruptly stopping shooting dope are better people than I am. No words can adequately describe the physical and mental torture I went through trying to walk away from heroin. In the end, I realized that I just couldn't do it on my own. I began exploring treatment facilities, albeit, not wholeheartedly. Any procrastinating that I was doing would come to a crashing halt when I got a little help in my decision-making process from the federal government.

Nearly seven months after bribing my way out of an arrest for the bank check thefts, the FBI decided they were going to take over the case. After an investigation and secret grand jury indictments, my crew and I were going to be prosecuted in federal court for numerous counts of conspiracy to steal mail matter, each count punishable by five years in a federal penitentiary. This didn't include state charges of forgery. I was looking at more than two hundred years in prison, but I had planned for such an eventuality. I had done the one smart thing that would save me from a lengthy prison sentence—I never signed any of the checks.

❋ ❋ ❋

I pleaded not guilty, basically claiming ignorance. I maintained that while I did in fact drive the crew from place to place, I was just that, a driver, and not involved in the stealing, forging, or cashing of the checks.

The FBI had me write handwriting exemplars for hours, comparing them to the signatures on the checks. After they determined that none of the forged signatures were mine, they had no choice but to believe me.

After an arrest such as this one, where multiple people are involved, it's every man for himself when it comes to a defense. Mine was plausible, and my crew didn't confirm or deny my account. They were too busy coming up with their own bullshit story. In the end, I got six months in the Metropolitan Correctional Center, the federal jail in Lower Manhattan. From my cell window, I could see the buildings I had ripped off. My crew averaged two years each, after a plea bargain. Not bad considering what they had each profited.

I admitted to the judge at sentencing that I was a heroin addict, and he gave me three months to clean up before I reported to jail. The feds mandated that I enter an established rehab facility and successfully complete the program. While they wouldn't hold my hand while I weaned myself off of drugs, they were the push I needed to get clean.

In addition, I needed to tell my kids what I'd done and where I was going. Even after the hardship of losing Tommy Ernst and the horrors of drug addiction, this would prove to be the toughest thing I'd ever lived through in my life.

I was forty-six years old, and I'd hit rock bottom.

11 Getting Clean

I had ninety days to get my act together. After I accomplished that, I could look forward to six months in a federal prison, but it would be a lot easier to endure without a heroin jones. I'd worry about telling my kids that I was going to jail after I'd unhooked myself. First things first.

I was in pretty bad shape. I'd lost considerable weight, and my complexion was death-pallid. My days were spent either high or waiting to get high. I knew that I was taking my life in my hands going to the East Village to cop heroin, but I didn't care. If the next fix was in hell, I'd gladly make the journey.

In the 1980s, the Lower East Side was the closest thing to the Black Hole of Calcutta as you could get. The squalor, mostly fueled by heroin and the emerging crack epidemic, was rampant. Violent crime was the norm; no one who lived there was unaffected by it. The NYPD's Ninth Precinct covered the worst: Avenues A, B, C, and D (Alphabet City).

I'd get stopped constantly by cops wanting to know what I was doing in the neighborhood. A white redhead was distinctly out of place. I took to carrying an address book. Whenever I was questioned, I'd look in the book and tell the cops that I was looking for an address and was lost. The streets ran alphabetically from east to west, and numerically from north to south. A person would have to be a moron to get lost in that area, but the excuse always worked for me. A short skirt and a smile didn't hurt, either.

My supplier was located in a dilapidated building on East Third Street. No matter what time of the day I went there, the place was dark and smelly. Candles were strategically placed at various points in the building for illumination; there was no electricity or running water. This was not an abandoned building; families lived there, and worse, paid rent to a slumlord who called Scarsdale home.

The dealer lived on the top floor of the four-story walk-up. He had the best shit, a potent product he bagged with the imprint "7-Up." I never went there when there weren't at least fifteen people waiting in line. I would be the only white female. On my worst days, I'd pay ten bucks to get to the head of the line.

After what seemed like hours, I'd get to an apartment door and slip my money through a slot, and out would come the dope. No friendly banter, commentary on the weather, no words exchanged at all.

By this time, I'd learned how to inject myself, overcoming my fear of needles with the reality of saving the four dollars I was paying Cleveland to do it for me. I could put that money toward my next fix. Very cost effective, I thought.

Depending on the shape I was in, I'd either shoot up right there in the hallway or wait until I got in my car, sometimes driving and shooting at the same time. Now there's an art form. I'd steer with my knees, tie off, cook and shoot, all while sailing along at 50 mph down the Brooklyn-Queens Expressway.

I don't know how I didn't get arrested or killed. One time, a platoon of uniformed cops stormed up the stairs while I was in line–just two customers away from my bags–and the stampede for freedom was on. Fortunately the cops' main concern was raiding the dealer's apartment, but we all knew that once the door came down, a few cops would come after us.

I ran like hell down the stairs behind a skinny Hispanic guy. He was yelling at the top of his lungs for someone to open a door. A woman in an apartment on a first floor complied, and both he and I spilled into the place. I was so close behind him that he didn't know that I had entered the apartment in his shadow.

When he turned and saw me, he said, "What the fuck are you doing here?"

"Same thing you are," I said breathlessly, "running from the cops."

It turned out that he lived there with his wife and son. A hardened junkie, he wanted to be as close to the product as possible.

He was moving for the back window. "We gotta get out of here."

"Shouldn't we cop first?"

That stopped him cold. I had a point. Why would we run *away* from the drugs when we were both in desperate need of a fix? Toward that end, we cooled our heels for about twenty of the longest minutes of our lives until the cops left with their prisoners, after which another entrepreneur opened up shop on the second floor.

Ripoff artists were another constant worry. Prowling gangs of predators would wait outside the buildings where junkies went to cop and steal their newly purchased drugs. I can't remember how many times I would spot these mutts and bluff them out of snatching my dope.

I'd sail right past them with, "Detective Dee, Ninth Squad. Lay a fucking hand on me and you're in." The gang would part like a hooker's legs and let me by.

Such is the life of a junkie in New York.

❀ ❀ ❀

I was determined to quit, not only because the feds had mandated it, but because I knew that it was either clean up or eventually die, get busted, or both.

Local hospitals ran rehabilitation clinics and detox centers all over Staten Island. The cost of treatment was free to anyone who had a Medicaid card. I didn't have one, but could have applied and been granted a card because of my addiction. Doing that, however, would have alerted the New York State Liquor Authority because I still held a liquor license, just no bar window to hang it in. Getting an SLA license in New York is tougher than finding an honest politician, and I wasn't about to give it up. Maybe one day I'd go back into the business.

I put the word out on the street that I was looking for a clean Medicaid card. Within a day, a local wiseguy stopped by my house.

This character *aspired* to be a wannabe, so low was he on the mob's career ladder. He looked like Robert De Niro in the movie *Mean Streets.*

"Yo, Terri, I got a virgin Medicaid card for you."

"How much?"

He looked perplexed. I guess he hadn't given it much thought. "I dunno. Fifty bucks?"

"Where's the card?"

He fished around in his wallet, and handed me a

fresh-looking card. I examined it to make sure it wasn't a forgery. All I needed was a federal forgery bust.

"Hey, it's real," he said, his pride apparently bruised. "Some broad musta lost it."

"Yeah, great," I said, "but do I look like Julie Love?"

"Huh?"

"The name on the card, Julie Love. Sounds like a black hooker."

"Probably is. You want it or not?"

I paid him. I was desperate.

❀ ❀ ❀

I signed myself into detox at Stapleton Hospital, telling my family that I had a job in Florida for ninety days.

"What kind of a job lasts ninety days?" my mother asked.

"I'm assembling air conditioners. It's seasonal." My mother would believe anything.

"Have a good time, dear. Write."

Detoxification was mandatory before I'd be assigned to a rehab facility. It was a seven-day program that basically tried to wean junkies off heroin with the aid of a few kind words and an occasional glass of orange juice. Pure torture.

I must have sweated a gallon of water an hour. My hair was matted with perspiration. The physical pain was almost unbearable, stomach cramps that made childbirth seem easy. On top of all that, the staff must have thought that I was a moron because I never answered to my name, which, if you remember, was now Julie Love. A nurse would be standing practically on top of me addressing me as "Julie," and I'd be on another planet.

187

There were some lighter moments. A fairly high-level wiseguy signed himself in for a heroin detox and wanted his two bodyguards to keep him company for the weeklong stay. When a staff member told him that it was against the hospital's policy to allow anyone other than drug-dependent patients on the premises, the mobster's two gorillas swore on paper that they were junkies just so they could keep their boss company. He sweated and writhed in pain while they commiserated and tried to distract him with endless games of pinochle.

When my week was up and I "graduated," I was told by the administrator that I was being sent to a rehab facility in Massachusetts because there were no beds available in New York.

"And how am I supposed to get up there?" I asked. I was too weak to drive and didn't trust myself to successfully navigate an airport terminal. If I walked more than fifteen yards, I needed to catch my breath. Detox had knocked me for a loop.

"We provide transportation," the administrator said.

What they supplied was a chauffeured limousine, paid for by the taxpayers of New York. A sleek black Cadillac picked me up and delivered me to the rehab center, located in a sleepy little town, four hours later.

The place was palatial by anyone's standards: spacious lawns, a pool, and private rooms. There was a New York wing where all the junkies from the Apple lived. The food was decent, and the staff catered to our needs around the clock. Two months there would be like a vacation. My only complaint was that I had to attend two twelve-step meetings every day, but I lived with it.

Ironically, it was easier to get drugs inside the facility than on the streets of Alphabet City. Visitors smuggled the stuff in. About half the patients were shooting dope on a daily basis. Some patients were making thousands of dollars a week selling various drugs to other patients. I kept my mouth shut and stayed clean, determined to beat my habit. With all that dope around, it wasn't easy.

After three weeks, I was told that a bed had been freed up in New York City, and I was being transferred for the remainder of my program. I hated to leave, but I had no choice. My chauffeur showed up the next day, and I reluctantly began my journey back to Manhattan.

I was clean and beginning to regain my strength and endurance and chatted it up with the driver on the way back to New York.

"Where're we going exactly?" I asked.

"I'm supposed to drop you off at the office at Grand Central Station. They'll assign you from there."

He ran his business out of his house in Brooklyn and gave me his card in case I ever needed a limo. Good thing I held onto it; I was going to need it.

He dropped me off at the office. I waited more than two hours before the clerical staff got my paperwork organized. A young woman shoved an ID card at me.

"Miss Love?" she said.

No response. "Oh...yes." I couldn't get used to that name.

"You're to report to this place," she handed me a three-page form, "in two hours."

I looked at the address. "This is the Bowery."

The Bowery is the last stop for junkies and alcoholics on their way to Potter's Field for an ignominious burial with four others in the same hole in the ground.

She smiled. "Your bed's waiting."

❋ ❋ ❋

I was in a shelter, sharing space with hard-core junkies, prostitutes, alcoholics, and homeless women. The place was filthy and reeked of urine and a few odors I couldn't identify. There was one bathroom and shower per forty women. I was issued a blanket and pointed to a cubbyhole with no door that was to be my living space for the next two months. A ceiling fan sat motionless above the sagging cot I'd been assigned. I turned it on as much to move the stale air as to dispense some of the smells. Then I sat down and sobbed.

A few minutes into my crying jag, I felt something falling onto my head. I thought it might be rain from a leaky roof and ran a hand through my hair. I dislodged at least five roaches. I screamed and jumped up. There had to be at least forty roaches riding the fan's blades and falling off at regular intervals like little skydivers.

I had to get out of there.

I got to a pay phone and called the chauffeur who had driven me from Massachusetts. Tears rolled from my eyes as I waited for someone to pick up. How much lower could I go? I had no one to call other than a total stranger because I hadn't confided to anyone that I was in rehab.

Within an hour, he was idling in front of the shelter.

I marched out of the building, hopped in the Caddy, and said, "Back to Mass."

"Why?"

"No beds. Someone screwed up."

He turned around and smiled. "Sure. I'll swear to it."

They took me back into the Massachusetts facility, no questions asked, but I'm sure they knew that I was lying about the paperwork snafu. As long as the good New York taxpayers were paying the freight, they didn't care. I'd be just another billable recovering junkie.

I was a model patient, attending meetings, cooperating with my shrink, and treating everyone with respect. The new me. I also was able to understand for the first time that my weakness toward addiction was a disease probably inherited from my alcoholic mother. I was determined to never again go near drugs or booze, a goal that met with limited success over the years.

❋　❋　❋

I was released from the program after ninety days, clean and sober. My lawyer got me an additional sixty days with my family before I had to report to jail because I was a single parent. I wanted to spend every minute of it with my sons.

My worst fear was that since I was back in my old environment, I might slip back into being a user. The temptation was enormous. Quite frankly, I didn't think I could remain straight on my own. I knew that Nicki and Margo would drop whatever they were doing and see me through this difficult time, but they were part of the lifestyle that I was trying to leave behind.

I had a friend of many years named Vinny Rizzo who lived in Florida. He had told me many times over the years that if I ever needed anything, I shouldn't hesitate to call him. If there was ever a time that I needed stability and guidance in my life, it was the weeks immediately following my release from rehab.

Vinny was what my family and mobbed-up friends would call a "citizen." He was in his forties, divorced, with a twenty-two-year-old son. Vinny owned a Great Bear auto repair shop in Miami and was as legitimate as Mr. Rogers. We were involved romantically at one time, but the relationship had evolved into one of friendship and respect. He had wanted more, but at that time, I was still in my wild-woman stage. In hindsight, had I stayed with Vinny, I would have probably led a clean, sedate life, and the closest I would've gotten to a mob would have been at the mall on Saturdays.

I called him and related how I'd screwed up my life, culminating in the battle to stay off heroin. Within three days, he was in New York catering to my every emotional need. He contacted a doctor friend of his who specialized in treating drug addiction. After several visits and intense counseling, I was confident that I could stay away from heroin, despite my environment.

As the weeks passed, I felt myself becoming closer to Vinny. We became intimate again, and although I'd sworn never to get serious with another man, I was slipping into love.

Vinny was a caring, emotional, giving man. Good looking didn't hurt, either. There was nothing that he wouldn't do for me or my boys. As it came closer to my time to turn myself in to begin my jail sentence, we began talking about our future together after I got out.

"Would you consider moving to Florida with me, Terri?" he asked, brown eyes twinkling.

I had known for a while that the question was coming. My sons were grown and self-sufficient;

Lenny was a reporter for the *Staten Island Advance*; the twins, Frank and Ronnie, were working their way through college. If I really loved Vinny, I had no excuse. To reject a truly decent man because I was hurt in the past or had made the wrong choices was foolish.

"There's nothing to consider," I said. "I'll go." Just saying the words gave me such a feeling of relief and pleasure. For years I had been denying myself the gratification of being happy. In retrospect, I believe now that I continued to use heroin to ease my emotional pain and my feeling of isolation.

Marriage wasn't discussed. Vinny knew how I felt about the subject. Besides, I was still legally married to Tony DeLorenzo. Neither of us had any desire to remarry, so we had never bothered filing for divorce.

Vinny and I experienced the joy of making plans for the future. His uncle would run the business in Florida while Vinny would remain in New York and visit me in jail as often as possible. His son, Vincent Jr., flew up for a visit. The last time I'd seen him, he was in elementary school. We got along fabulously.

As the date when I had to report to MCC neared, I dreaded having to tell my sons that their mother was going to jail. The impact of that revelation would be softened by Vinny's being around. The boys really liked him. And while I dreaded the confrontation, I was looking toward the future when I got out and resumed a normal life. My new orderly world, however, would soon come crashing down.

❀ ❀ ❀

February 23, 1982. Vinny and I had driven to the local market for groceries. We had rented a condo on Staten Island and needed some extra provisions because Vinny's son had returned for a second visit. I was to report to prison in two weeks, and we were inseparable, trying to make every minute special before I had to go. Six months in jail might not seem like very long unless you're the one doing the time and separated from those you love.

It was a warm day for the middle of winter, about fifty-five and sunny. Vinny parked the car and honked a greeting to his son, who was in our apartment on the second floor. As I opened the trunk, I saw Vincent Jr. slide open the terrace door and wave. I grabbed a bag of freshly baked bagels, the aroma reminding me that I had skipped breakfast.

The doors of a battered Ford Fairlane parked across the street swung open. Two men in their thirties wearing leather jackets stepped out and began walking swiftly toward us. Vinny was waving to his son and was oblivious to their presence. I felt the distinct chill of trouble. My throat constricted; my heart sank. When both men were about ten feet from Vinny, one of them shouted, "Hey, Rizzo!" and they both reached into their waistbands.

I dropped the bag of bagels. "No!" I screamed. "Vinny, run!"

He had turned toward the men at the sound of his name, a silly grin on his face. As I shouted, he turned toward me, apparently confused at the urgency in my voice. His jaw dropped when he saw my face, and he turned back to the men.

Both had drawn revolvers and opened fire simultaneously. A gush of air shot from Vinny as he was hit four times in the chest. He staggered a few steps toward our building and collapsed in the street. I whirled and ran down the block screaming. Two bullets whizzed past me.

I turned briefly to see one of the men standing

over Vinny. He fired two bullets into the back of his head. Vincent Jr., now fully exposed on the terrace, was wailing, "I love you, Dad!" As long as I live, I'll never forget him shrieking those words.

I stopped running, but continued to back down the street. The two men calmly walked back to their car and drove off. My legs felt like they were anchored to the ground, but I managed to get to Vinny as his blood seeped into the gutter. Neighbors were pouring into the street. Vinny's son was screaming for his dad from the terrace.

Time appeared to stand still. People were moving in slow motion. I heard the muffled pitch of a police siren. People were talking to me, asking if I was okay. Their voices reverberated like I was in an echo chamber.

Vinny was dead, his eyes wide open in stunned disbelief. I knelt beside him, holding his hands and waiting for the tears to come, but none did. Either I was in a deep state of shock or I'd gotten inured to violence over the years. Maybe a combination of both. I just sat in the gutter in a pool of blood and brain matter, cradling Vinny's head in my hands and wishing that the bullets fired at me had found their mark.

The same cops that had responded to Tommy Ernst's shooting were the first to arrive on the scene. They recognized me immediately and looked at me with dropped jaws.

All I could think to say to them was, "Why me?" Vinny lay dead at my feet, and I was wondering why the people that I loved had a habit of being murdered in front of me.

The next three days were a blur. It was Tommy Ernst's funeral revisited. If there was ever a time where I'd be sorely tempted to go back to heroin, the weeks immediately after Vinny's murder certainly qualified. But I stayed clean.

Despite being depressed and in deep mourning, I tried to fathom why anyone would want to kill Vinny Rizzo. The man had never even gotten a parking ticket, let alone had a criminal record or consorted with criminals. No one in his family was remotely connected to organized crime.

The police were perplexed, too, but a week after the funeral, the investigating detective called to tell me that three days prior to the murder, Vinny had gotten into an altercation in a local bar. What amounted to a pushing and shoving match was quickly stopped by the bar's owner, who tossed everyone out.

The argument began when Vinny had returned from the men's room to find a twenty-dollar bill missing from his change on the bar. The bartender gave a surreptitious nod toward two men who had been sitting next to Vinny, but who had moved to the end of the bar.

Words led to accusations and shoves that continued on the street after the three were ejected. The two men were drunk, and Vinny was sober; I'd never known him to take more than three drinks at a sitting. What transpired on the street is unknown; there were no witnesses. Whatever happened, Vinny couldn't have thought too much of it because he never mentioned the incident to me. Just your run-of-the-mill bar dispute.

The men were first-timers in the bar. The police had the bartender confer with a department artist. A pretty good rendering of the men was shown around the neighborhood and distributed to all police precincts. I took copies to my family for circulation to their associates to see if the two were connected. Nothing ever came of either investigation, and Vinny's murder remains unsolved. The police wrote it off as Vinny confronting the wrong people being in the wrong place at the wrong time. What should have ended on the street in front of the bar festered into Vinny's murder by men who held a grudge.

※ ※ ※

I was permitted an extension on my reporting date to jail. People in "the life" never have anything good to say about law enforcement officials, but I have nothing but praise for the way they treated me during my time of mourning. They gave me the time to decompress and make certain that my family was cared for while I was away.

My boys were men now, but I wanted someone around whom they were familiar with and could talk to if they needed anything. I didn't want to burden my family, feeling ashamed of myself for disgracing the Dee name. Besides, my father and uncles were getting old, and my mother's alcoholism had made her useless as someone who could be relied upon.

I turned to Tony DeLorenzo, my estranged husband, primarily because I had nowhere else to turn and because I trusted him with the boys. A thief and a liar, most certainly, but as he once told me, "It doesn't make me a bad person." And he was right, he still had a place in his heart for me and my boys, as I did for him. He was in Florida, playing the ponies and whatever else could run a race and lose. I called him and told him the whole sordid story.

"I need you, Tony. I need you to look after my family."

No hesitation. "I'll be up tomorrow."

He flew up the next day as promised. Now with one week until I reported to jail, I had to talk to my sons. I thought I was scared when I had my sit-down with Jimmy Red, but telling my boys that I was going to jail, and worse, *why* I was going to jail, would be the toughest sit-down of my life.

❀ ❀ ❀

My boys looked like Tom Selleck, and that's not just a mother talking. The three younger boys could pass for triplets, strapping young men with shoulder-length dark hair, moustaches, and chiseled features. Their dark complexions were made more pronounced by the tans they'd acquired from outdoor sports. My son, John, was a bull, very muscular and solid like my father. He had joined the navy and had written me recently that he had volunteered for SEAL training. He would subsequently enter BUDs, the SEAL training school, pass with flying colors, and complete ten years in the navy before returning to civilian life.

My boys who were still at home, young men or not, were still my babies. Looking back on their upbringing, I realized that I was a pretty good mother, but I had a lot of guilt for the years I'd abused drugs and raised them by the seat of my pants. I had attended school functions, ball games, and family gatherings while I was high, often waking up the next day with the realization that I'd blacked out the previous day's events. I might as well have not gone at all. For those years, I'm deeply ashamed.

We were gathered in the living room, my sons seated on the couch and me standing before them.

I let out a deep breath. "I've got something to tell you." They waited, and I told them the entire story, leaving nothing out. I broke down near the end.

At first they just stared at me. I didn't know what to make of it. The boys were strong, the legacy of the Dees, but now they looked like they were in shock. Just coming off of Vinny's murder, I didn't know how they were going to react.

"I'm sorry," I blubbered. They bounced off the couch and rushed to me. It was a group hug, like something out of a bad sitcom. Tears all around.

It was over. I felt more relief than I'd experienced in years. The fear that my boys would abandon me was always in the back of my mind. A convicted felon and a junkie at that. Who would've blamed them?

After we had regained our composure, Ronnie said, "We'll come and visit you as often as we can." Frank and Lenny agreed. They'd be there every day if they could.

"I don't want you to visit me," I said. I'd given this a lot of thought. I didn't want my children seeing their mother while separated by an inch of Plexiglas.

They protested vehemently, but I had the final say. It would kill me not to be able to see or touch them for six months, but I didn't want them to remember me like that: a prisoner, stripped of my dignity.

I needed a drink so badly I thought I was going to burst. Instead, I went to the kitchen and downed two glasses of ice water. I was emotionally spent. When I got back to the living room, Lenny said, "We'll write every day."

I felt the tears coming again, but I smiled through them.

"You're damn right you will."

❀　❀　❀

I took a taxi to jail. I didn't want my family anywhere around when the cell door slammed behind me. I stopped at my parents' house on the way to Manhattan. They met me at the door. My father took my departure the hardest.

"I failed you, Tiger." He'd known the day was coming, but how does a parent prepare himself for the day his only daughter goes to prison?

I hugged him. "I failed myself, Daddy." The three of us went to the kitchen, the epicenter of every Italian home.

My mother, sober for once, made coffee, and we visited like the typical American family I knew we weren't. With the cabdriver waiting, and the time I had to report etched in granite, my visit was short.

As the cab pulled away, my parents remained in front of the house, waving feebly. I was suffering more for my parents than I was for myself. For them, the blame game must be going into extra innings.

The cabdriver looked over his shoulder. "Where to now, lady?"

"You know where MCC is in Manhattan?"

"Downtown, right?"

"Yeah, we're going there."

He turned toward the Verrazano Bridge. It was a gorgeous June day, one of the few times in New York when the sky was achingly clear and blue and the clouds were pillowy and pure white.

"You got a boyfriend in there or something?"

I continued to gaze out the window. "Or something."

12 Queen of MCC

I never really knew fear. Even when Tommy Ernst and Vinny Rizzo were gunned down right before my eyes, I wasn't scared; it was more like shock. When a person fears, they fear for their life, their safety. Fear is a breach of control. What you cannot control, you fear. This is the reason behind a lot of people's fear of flying. It's not the height; it's the fact that you trust your life to a pilot, and you have no control over how he or she flies the plane.

Fear was always an emotion that was completely foreign to me. Granted, this is a reckless attitude, primarily enjoyed by the young and stupid (usually synonymous words). As a teenager, you think you're invincible; hardly a revelation, we all know this. But as a person gets on in years, the reality of death becomes more omnipresent. We become more fearful of common everyday activities. Kids evade vehicular traffic like they're playing dodge ball; old people are afraid to cross the street. Fear creeps up on us in chronological degrees.

It never crept up on me. Believe me, I'm not bragging about it. If I was more fearful, I wouldn't have led the reckless life that I did. I wouldn't have become a junkie. Hell, I wouldn't have gotten involved in stealing checks or even in owning a bar. But finally, at the age of forty-six, I learned fear for the first time. I went to jail.

When that steel door slammed behind me minutes after I arrived, I knew what real fear was. The world I knew was a million miles away, yet it surrounded me in the downtown neighborhood that housed the Metropolitan Correctional Center.

I was not in control. From the minute I got up in the morning until the lights went out at night, I had no power over my actions. I was told when to eat, sleep, and shower. I was told what I could read and watch on television. I was to have no independent thought. I was just to follow directions blindly.

It scared the hell out of me.

❊ ❊ ❊

The intake process was degrading. I was ushered into a holding cell where I was stripped and body cavity searched. I gave up my clothes and was issued a shirt, pants, towel, one pillow, and one sheet. A female corrections officer led me to an administrative office where another bored CO read me a list of the prison rules, handing me a printed copy in case I had a memory lapse.

The corrections officers were like prisoners themselves. My first thought upon seeing them was to wonder if they had lives beyond the prison walls. They had the same thousand-mile stare that the cons had; the vacant expression of someone who has seen every nasty thing the world has to offer. I was to find out that there was a shortage of guards, both male and female. It wasn't out of the norm for a guard to work double and triple shifts, often not leaving the institution for a week at a time.

A corrections officer had to balance the job of enforcing the rules against surviving in a hostile environment. They would overlook some infractions, enforce others, walking the tightrope that ensured their survival. Keeping a lid on the most aggressive prisoners had to be tempered against doing the bare minimum to keep order and stay alive.

I was taken by yet-another CO to my new home, a cell on the sixth floor that was referred to as a "room" because there was a steel door in place of the traditional bars.

My room measured about twelve-by-seven. It was furnished with a steel bed with a paper-thin mattress, an irritating wool blanket, a commode with no lid, a sink, and a chair. I was permitted to have my own radio. The walls and ceiling were painted olive drab, most of it peeling. Be it ever so crumbled....

I had a window. Talk about your amenities. About the size of the *Daily News*, it was made of wire-reinforced thick glass that could repel a how-itzer round. Just to be on the safe side, tempered steel bars ran along the inside sill. I had a view of the neighborhood that housed the brokerage firms that I'd ripped off.

Lights out was at 11 PM. COs would enter the cells about an hour later, carrying rubber mallets, wake up the prisoners, and bang on the window bars to make certain that they were intact. A peaceful night's sleep was not possible.

The food was abysmal. We rose at 6 AM for breakfast, marched to a dining room in the basement, and filed past a few prisoner cooks who handed us trays. Normal breakfast fare consisted of one egg, powdered or hard-boiled, a piece of dry toast, an envelope of instant coffee, a cup of hot water, and, if we were lucky, a container of orange juice. Lunch was either the most horrible-smelling meatloaf I've ever come across or some sort of mystery stew, with powdered potatoes and canned veggies. Dinner wasn't much better. I hated the slop they served us, but forced a little down so the hacks (corrections officers—I picked up the con lingo very quickly) wouldn't think I was on a hunger strike and force-feed me.

For the first week, I spent the entire time in my cell, except for meals, usually with a blanket over my head wallowing in self-pity or listening to the radio. A television was located in a community room on the fifth floor, but I wasn't interested.

I soon realized that I either had to buck up or someone was going to hand my head to me. Granted, I was in the women's wing, but female cons can be just as vicious as males. The weak are singled out for exploitation, and I wasn't about to let that happen to me. I had already been seeing the signs: a shove here and there on the food line, someone pushing ahead of me for the pay phone. If I didn't assert myself, I was going to get hurt. Jail is like Dodge City without the heroes.

The women on my floor were serving time for a variety of crimes. The most dangerous were the Colombian mules—women who had gotten locked up for transporting cocaine from South America, usually for their boyfriends—and a handful of Black Panthers and Black Liberation Army co-conspirators who were serving hard time, mostly for conspiracy to murder cops and for bank robbery. There was also a group of Weather Underground anarchists, but they kept pretty much to themselves.

I had to align myself with one of the groups; there's no such thing as a loner in prison, at least not a healthy one. I chose the Colombians because they were more cunning. All this amounted to was being friendly and not asking too many questions. Later, when I finagled a job in the kitchen, I'd supply them with fresh vegetables and fruit, commodities they appreciated. In return, they watched my back and told me if I was going to be singled out for a potential ass whipping.

The BLA and Panther inmates were constantly being called before federal grand juries to testify, and when they refused, even though they were granted immunity, they were slapped with additional eighteen-month sentences. These people weren't going anywhere for quite a while, and they were very pissed off, particularly at the white establishment. Since they couldn't assault a judge or prosecutor, any white person would do, yours truly being a great target of opportunity.

I began to act tough. I developed a swagger and a "fuck you" attitude. The tougher and crazier the other prisoners thought you were, the further away they stayed. If I finished my sentence without making one friend, I would consider it time well spent.

Still, I was tested. A black dyke with arms like tree trunks decided one day that she wanted to use the same clothes dryer that I was using and began tossing my damp clothes on the floor, claiming that I'd dumped out her stuff first.

I was scared witless, but confronted her anyway.

"Put my fucking things back in the dryer," I said, fists balled to keep my hands from shaking. There were four other prisoners in the laundry room, but no hacks. The dyke had her girlfriend with her, a very slight, pretty black woman. I had two Colombians watching my back. One of them passed me a sock stuffed with a crumpled bar of soap, a very effective weapon.

We faced off for a few seconds, and the dyke backed off.

There was an outdoor gym on the roof of the prison. The area was enclosed by barbed-wire walls and a razor-wire roof. There were several Universal machines for our use, and I tried to get up there every day.

One day, I went to the gym to find six black women, all BLA or Panther members, using the equipment. As soon as I realized that I was the only white woman on the roof, I had two choices: turn around and leave or show some spunk and stay. I chose the latter, the former being a sign of weakness that I would have had to pay for. I stayed and worked out, waiting my turn on a machine when I had to. I kept my mouth shut, finished my workout, and left. My sweats and bandana headband were soaked through from more than the usual perspiration developed during exercise. But I gained the grudging respect of the black prisoners, and they kept their distance from me. I reciprocated.

❋ ❋ ❋

I was in MCC for about a month when a hack brought a white shoebox to me in my room.

"What the hell's this?"

The hack, an older white woman I'll call Maggie, whispered conspiratorially, "Open it, you'll like what you find."

A word here about the hacks. We had only female guards, which made sense, but they could be as easily corrupted as the male guards. Prisoners had access to just about every illegal substance and activity that was available on the outside. A prisoner could get drugs, place a bet, drink liquor. I'd even heard that hookers were being smuggled up to the wiseguys on the eleventh floor. If it wasn't for the guards looking the other way to maintain the status quo, or getting a piece of the action themselves, none of this could be permitted.

Maggie put the box on my bed, said, "Enjoy," and left.

I was like a kid on Christmas morning. I popped open the lid. What I found was better than drugs or money or booze; it was the next best thing to a pass out of there.

A sandwich.

A big, fat, Carnegie Deli-type of sandwich, packed three inches high with rare, hot roast beef, dripping with mayonnaise, all packed neatly between two slices of real Jewish rye bread. And oh yes, a kosher dill pickle on the side.

I'd lost considerable weight because I couldn't stomach the crappy food. I'm not that picky; I'll shovel down a White Castle hamburger or a hot dog just like anyone else, but the garbage that they served us gave new meaning to the term "cruel and unusual punishment."

For a split second, I wondered what mysterious benefactor would smuggle such a treat in to me. Then I did a one-eighty and considered who might want to poison me. Almost immediately, I thought, fuck it, if I'm gonna die, so be it.

I picked up the sandwich, closed my eyes, and took a huge bite. Heaven. At that moment if Robert Redford had come into my room with his dick in his hand and said, "Terri, this is for you," I'm afraid I would have had to tell him to stand at attention until I finished the roast beef.

I made the sandwich disappear in less than five minutes. David Copperfield would have been proud. I picked up the box hoping for a clue as to who sent the food (or to maybe find dessert). On the bottom of the white box was a white piece of paper, folded over once. I opened it to find a handwritten note.

"Terri: Enjoy the sandwich? We need to talk.

—Tony Pro"

❋ ❋ ❋

Tony Provenzano was about sixty and a capo in the Genovese family who was doing time for racketeering and murder. He also controlled the Teamsters Union. I'd never met him, but my father called him The Magician because he was rumored to have been responsible for the disappearance of Jimmy Hoffa. He'd also allegedly made his boss, Tony Bender, vanish. Tony Pro was a very powerful, vicious person who was housed on the eleventh floor with the other wiseguys. Why he wanted to see me, or better yet, how he was going to be able to see me, was a mystery. Men and women were strictly segregated. The eleventh floor might as well have been on Mars; there was no way I could imagine that we were going to get together. While I was pondering why and how, Maggie reappeared.

"Come with me," she said.

I followed her to the stairway and down we went, past checkpoints and smiling hacks, right to the basement level where the kitchen was located.

It was about 3 PM, between meals, and the kitchen was empty except for a skeleton crew of prisoners cleaning the dining area, with a male hack watching over them.

Maggie pointed to the pantry.

"You go in there. I'll wait here."

The hack guarding the cleaners completely ignored me. I opened the door to the pantry and slipped inside.

Tony Pro was sitting at a table sipping from a Styrofoam cup. He smiled.

"Terri, come here, sit. Enjoy the sandwich?"

I went to the table and sat. "Yes, thanks." I didn't dare ask where he got it.

Tony smiled. For a con, he was very well groomed; manicure, good haircut. "I know your father."

"That's nice. What am I doing here?"

He ignored the question. "You want coffee? Maybe some wine? Scotch?"

"Huh?"

He got up, went to a big cupboard, reached behind it, and came out with a bottle of Red Label. He flipped a coffee cup that was on a drain, poured two fingers, and handed it to me.

Screw it. I downed it in one gulp, and it immediately went to my head. It was a good feeling.

"Listen, we run this place," he said. "Any friend of ours has a problem, we fix it."

I shook my head. "I don't have a problem."

"Sure you do, we all do. The food sucks."

As the Scotch worked its way through my system, I began to relax. I hadn't had a drink in months, and I had little tolerance.

"What can I do about that?" I asked.

"Plenty. Your old man once told me that you were a helluva cook, right?"

I enjoyed cooking, it relaxed me, and I was very good at it. "Yeah, so? What good is that going to do me—us—here?"

"The joint's looking for a kosher cook because of the BLA and Panther assholes. They're all Muslims. Court order. They gotta eat kosher, part of their religion or some shit."

I knew that MCC only allowed male cooks. They didn't want men and women fraternizing. Besides, I wasn't Jewish. I didn't think I needed to explain any of this to Tony Pro, but I did anyway. The booze talking.

"Sonny knows the hack that handles the personnel files," Tony said, referring to Sonny Francese, a gangster doing ninety-nine years for bank robbery. "Your religion's been changed to Jewish. You got the job."

I laughed out loud. "You gotta be kidding." Dalessio a Jew? Next thing I knew, Schwartz would be Chinese.

He got serious. "I don't kid when it comes to my stomach. It cost us, but you're in. Starting tomorrow, things are gonna change around here."

And change they did. For the first time in the history of the federal penal system, a female prisoner would become a cook alongside male prisoners. If that wasn't enough, I was officially a Jew. *Mazel tov.*

❊   ❊   ❊

The next morning, I was awakened at 4 AM, two hours before the rest of the prisoners, and brought down to the kitchen by a female hack I'd never seen before.

The kitchen staff, about fifteen men, were already hard at work. They looked at me like hungry wolves, but went back to work when I glared at the ugliest of the lot. The hack handed me to another hack, this one male, who told me that I'd find a change of clothes in the pantry.

I changed into whites and a pair of black combat boots with reinforced steel toes. In case I dropped something heavy on my feet, I'd be protected, and the boots would certainly come in handy if I needed to kick someone in the groin. I planned to cook, not get raped.

I acclimated quickly. For the first few days, I did my job, which was to prepare kosher meals. I had the best ingredients to work with. The veggies were fresh from local supermarkets in Little Italy, the steaks were still mooing. Anything I wanted, I got, by order of the United States Supreme Court. The Muslims might have been bank-robbing, murdering sonsofbitches, but they got religion when they arrived at MCC and demanded their kosher meals. I had a free hand in menu preparation. I made tomato, meat, and Alfredo sauces, among other things. Lasagna was a specialty. The Muslims never ate so good.

At the end of the first week, I got a visit in the kitchen from a black guy nicknamed Cigar because he was tall and skinny. I had just tossed thirty pounds of linguine into three fifty-five gallon pots of boiling water.

Cigar, I noticed, was wearing a prison jumpsuit that was at least two sizes too big for him. He pulled ten plastic baggies from his pockets.

"Mr. Pro sent me. Fill 'em up."

I loaded the bags with the cooked pasta and sauce. Cigar took them into the pantry and came out looking like the Goodyear blimp. He had taped the baggies all over his body and sloshed when he walked.

"How're you gonna get that stuff up to the eleventh floor without being stopped?" I asked.

"The elevator, Sweet Cheeks, how the hell else?"

There was a hack assigned to the elevator, but he'd obviously been bought or just didn't give a damn.

I was supposed to prepare thirty-five dinners a night. When Cigar wasn't taping the evening's entree to his body, I'd prepare ten extra trays that would somehow get diverted to the boys upstairs. About three weeks into my new job, Tony Pro came downstairs to personally thank me. He'd easily gained ten pounds.

"Terri, you're making our time almost a pleasure."

I was stirring a pot of tomato sauce with a three-pound steel ladle. Soon my arms would be as big as the black dyke's who wanted to kick my ass. "Hey, whatever I can do." I was sorry I said it as soon as the words passed my lips. I saw the look in Tony's eyes. He had a scam planned, and I was going to be part of it.

"Your friend Rita's gonna visit you tomorrow."

"I don't have a friend named Rita."

He grinned. "You do now."

❋ ❋ ❋

The goombas weren't allowed to have contact visits. I wasn't either until I got the kosher cooking position. One of the bennies for successfully handling the extra responsibilities of running the kitchen.

The prison was still off-limits to my kids, but Tony DeLorenzo stopped by once a week. We'd meet in a community visiting room, hug and talk for twenty minutes or so, all under the watchful eyes of a half-dozen hacks. When Tony left, I'd be patted down. Once in a while, I'd get strip-searched. No big deal, I'd gotten used to being groped by butch hacks, a thrill for them, tolerated by me.

Rita, whoever the hell she was, was obviously going to pass something to me. I was scared. If caught with contraband, I could be charged with a crime, depending on what the swag was, and have more time tacked onto my sentence. But I wasn't foolish enough to tell Tony Provenzano that I wanted no part of it. For one, I owed him for my cooking job. Second, I had no desire to add to his reputation as The Magician by vanishing from my room in the middle of the night.

Rita was a Bensonhurst bimbette with big hair, big breasts, and a big ass, the favorite extracurricular-type plaything for married wiseguys. Their wives looked like Olympia Dukakis. Their bimbos resembled Fran Dresher on a bad hair day.

Rita was wearing enough makeup to disguise the Elephant Man, and when she hugged me like a long-lost sister, I cringed. Half her face rubbed off on my kitchen whites.

She babbled for ten minutes while I just nodded and smiled. The entire time she was there, all I could think about was doing an extra ten years for smuggling in a gram of cocaine.

Suddenly, she got up.

"Terri, honey, you look great. See you next week?"

"Yeah, sure," I said dumbly.

She hugged me, squeezed my hand, leaving a small lumpy envelope in it. As she turned to leave, I stuck the package in my bra. The hacks would have had to be blind not to have seen the move. Too late to worry about it. I walked to the checkpoint leading back to the kitchen on rubbery legs.

A butch hack who always volunteered to pat down the women inmates met me with a smile. A male guard stood by impassively.

"Raise 'em up, dear," she said with a leer.

I lifted my arms, and she expertly ran her hands over my body, lingering in all the wrong places. After she squeezed my breasts, she started to slide her hand into my bra.

The male hack spoke up. "Angie, that's all right. She's okay."

213

She backed off, clearly disappointed. "Okay, go on."

The male hack looked right through me like I wasn't there. Either he didn't want to see me get felt up by his colleague or he was on Tony's Pro's payroll; I never found out which. I locked the pantry door behind me and retrieved the envelope. It contained about a half-ounce of marijuana. Within an hour, Tony was in the kitchen picking up the grass.

He quickly stuffed it into his pocket. "You take any?"

I looked at him like he had two heads. "Hell, no. Do you take me for an idiot?" Steal from a boss? Did this guy think I had some kind of death wish?

"We're inside now, Terri. Take some, it's okay."

"That's okay." I waved him off, put my apron back on.

"Next time, then?"

There was going to be a next time? "Yeah, sure."

❊   ❊   ❊

Rita showed up like clockwork once a week, passing me an envelope every time. I was patted down, but nothing invasive.

I skimmed off what amounted to maybe four joints every visit. At first I smoked them, but soon tired of getting high alone. I also was feeling guilty for falling off the wagon. I don't know if I really wanted the grass or just wanted to use it up before my cell was tossed. A group of hacks we called the Mod Squad would raid prisoners' rooms unannounced and rip them apart looking for contraband. Nothing was sacred. They would dismantle sink pipes, shred sanitary napkins, any place or item that could hide the smallest amount of drugs or conceal a weapon.

I decided to go into the retail grass business. I wound up selling loose joints to inmates for five dollars each. After two months, Rita began dropping by twice a week and tripled the amount of marijuana she smuggled in. I was clearing $50 a day in the smoke trade, a far greater amount than the eighty-cent stipend the government allowed. I wouldn't take any cash. The money had to be deposited into my commissary account to be retrieved when I got out. But I was taking a chance storing the marijuana in my room, and I prayed that I wouldn't be the subject of a search by the Mod Squad.

My luck didn't last. I was roughly jostled out of sleep one morning at 2 AM. The Mod Squad stormed into my room in full force: five hacks in battle gear in the event that I resisted.

They tore the room apart, as expected, leaving without a word or helping me reassemble my room. The place was a mess, but who was I going to complain to?

But they missed the marijuana.

I had a cork-type bulletin board with printed recipes and index cards with meal schedules tacked to it. I'd hidden the grass behind a postcard someone had sent me from Florida, flattening out the baggie to the approximate size of the card and thumbtacking both to the board. The hacks ripped the board off the wall looking for contraband that I might have hidden behind it, but neglected to look under the individual cards and papers, probably thinking them too thin to hide anything.

✳ ✳ ✳

I continued in the drug trade, at the same time whipping up great meals in the kitchen. One of the wiseguys upstairs must have had a friend who owned a liquor store because after a while, the crates of beef that were delivered had bottles of Scotch and vodka layered underneath the meat. I'd smuggle some liquor to my room with Tony Pro's blessing, but watched my intake. I went from totally clean when I'd arrived at MCC to drinking and smoking grass. I could see my downfall coming when I was released and got scared, so I deluded myself into thinking that I could control my habits. Every addict's fantasy.

I was doing my time hassle free and after three months, was seeing the light at the end of the tunnel. Halfway home. If I had to be in prison, MCC was the place to do the time.

Then the bottom fell out.

✳ ✳ ✳

I was awakened at my usual hour, only this time by two hacks.

"What's up?" I asked sleepily.

"You're being transferred. Get dressed," one of them replied.

I swung my legs out of bed. "Huh? Transferred where?" I thought I was being moved to another room, another floor maybe.

"Alderson."

Alderson Federal Reformatory was a maximum-security prison for women in the mountains of West Virginia. What the hell did I do to deserve this? The hacks either didn't know or played dumb.

✳ ✳ ✳

I was given time to pack my meager belongings and have a nonkosher breakfast. Tony Pro and the rest of the wiseguys were in the dining room. I was the only female in a sea of seventy-five men. Two hacks stood over me while I ate.

I caught Tony's eye as I was being escorted from the dining room. I could swear that he was crying. The last time Tony Provenzano shed a tear was when a doctor slapped him on the ass and told his mother, "It's a boy!" Now the goombas on the eleventh floor would have to go back to prison fare. I'd be crying, too.

I was shackled hand and foot like Houdini, and I shuffled to a waiting van that had seen better days, the only prisoner going for a ride. I had a wooden bench all to myself. No one would answer any of my questions.

"What am I, the Birdwoman of Alcatraz? Why the sudden move?"

No response.

Two female hacks accompanied me; one drove, the other rode shotgun.

The trip took ten hours. The battered van barely made it. I was convinced that ballpoint-pen springs were being used as shock absorbers. I felt every bump in the road, but fortunately, we made frequent stops along the way. I remained shackled while I minced my way into highway rest-stop bathrooms to relieve myself. The hacks refused to unlock my restraints so I could pee; they pulled my pants down for me. How embarrassing.

I never found out for certain why I was whisked away from MCC. Being a fairly intelligent individual, I can speculate that my cooking arrangement with the wiseguys was uncovered, and in order to minimize a scandal that may have reached the media, I had to be isolated.

❊ ❊ ❊

For a maximum-security prison, Alderson was the plushest jail I'd ever seen. The facility was nestled in the mountains and consisted of numerous two-story buildings spread out over several hundred acres. I was assigned to a room, like at MCC, but this one had carpeting and a television. Inmates were permitted to leave their cells during the day and go to different buildings as long as they signed in and out so the hacks could monitor comings and goings.

Inmates who were ambulatory had to work. I was assigned a floor buffer. Others, like the Manson girls, who were in for murder and were a little flaky, didn't have to lift a finger. They kept to themselves and could be seen walking the grounds holding hands. Squeaky Fromm, who tried to assassinate President Gerald Ford, was an inmate in Alderson, too. She was a real whack job and spent most of her time medicated.

My room once housed Iva Toguri d'Aquino, aka Tokyo Rose. Her name was carved on the wall above my bed, dated July 1953. A little bit of history

I did the remainder of my time like a ghost. Drug dealing was rampant in the facility, but I chose not to get involved. I stomached the food; jail food is jail food unless you're the kosher cook. I never thought I'd be homesick for MCC.

I was released in November 1982, having served my time. During the bus ride home, I promised myself that from now on I'd lead the life of a "citizen." I assumed that jail had taught me a lesson.

I should have known myself better.

13 The Road to Ruin

Getting out of jail was like being reborn. I had a great reunion with my three oldest boys. (John was still in the Navy, stationed in Coronado, California.) Catching up took a day, the rest of the time was spent appreciating each other. The boys were doing fine. Tony had come through and been there for them. He had gotten a job in construction and was home every night, making sure that they had dinner together before the boys vanished to do whatever young men did. Tony stayed with us for a few weeks after my release, but I could tell that he was itching to get back to Florida.

"Winter's coming, Terri," he'd tell me several times a day. He was gone by the second week in November.

My primary concern was staying clean. I'd slipped a few times in prison, but jail is a controlled environment, and I knew that I couldn't go completely nuts and revert back to being a degenerate junkie. But now I was home, and my old friends and connections came calling.

Junkies naturally gravitate to other junkies. The

219

friends I'd had before I went away were now on the phone every day trying to get me back into the lifestyle. While they didn't intentionally try to reintroduce me to smack, they wanted me to stop by a local bar and have a few welcome-home drinks with them. I knew that if I did that, I'd be on the road to oblivion in no time. The urge to begin the party again was almost irresistible. Such is the draw of heroin. My solution: run away.

I decided that the only way to resist temptation was to flee from it. Florida seemed a safe haven. I called Vinny Mirabile, a strapping six-footer about my age, an old boyfriend who had headed south after he had beaten heroin. I called and told him of my plans. He wanted me to move in with him, but I declined. Vinny may have said that he kicked the habit, but I hadn't seen him in a while and couldn't take his word that he was drug free. Junkies are accomplished liars, and slipping back into the life is not unheard of. He arranged for a motel room, though, and I flew to Florida the next day. We saw each other socially, but I was leery of him and wouldn't commit to any type of relationship until I was certain that he was off heroin. Junkies can be good actors, too. I figured I could spend a few months there until I acclimated to my newly regained freedom and able to return home temptation free. I wound up staying for six years.

Before I made my move, I had to clear it with my parole officer. I had three years of supervised parole to do before I was totally free from the system. There were no "see and pees" in 1982, where cons get drug tested, all we had to do was report once a week to show that we were still breathing and gainfully employed. Some parole officers could be very hard nosed, but fortunately mine was a sweetheart, and he allowed me to make the move and report to his counterpart in Miami. All I had to do was find a job within a week of arriving in Florida.

This was a problem. There were plenty of jobs, but I didn't want to flip burgers or ask K-Mart shoppers how they were doing, and these types of menial positions were usually the only ones available to ex-cons. I was forbidden to work in any licensed establishment (bars, restaurants), so my pickings were limited. I was used to making good money, and I wanted something where I'd make a decent living.

Vinny, who was also between jobs, saw an ad in a newspaper for rental car transporters: "Big money for people who can hustle."

"What do you think a car transporter does?" Vinny asked.

"I haven't got the slightest, but I'm sure we'd be good at it."

We went to the address listed, a car rental warehouse, where cars were brought in from other states to be delivered to the various rental outlets throughout Florida. The job was simple enough; we were basically car jockeys, delivering cars wherever they were needed or returning cars to franchises after they were used for one-way rentals.

Vinny and I took the job and ran cars all over the state. The harder we worked, the more money we made, and we did pretty well. Vinny seemed to be steering clear of junk, so when he asked me to move in with him, I agreed.

Life was pretty good. We were making good money, I was reporting to my PO on time, and I was drug free. Of course, I had to come up with a way to screw things up and make some dishonest money. I wasn't happy unless I was working a scam. I had chastised Tommy Ernst for the same behavior, and now I'd joined the club. The easy cash I'd made stealing checks had poisoned me against legitimate hard work.

"There's got to be an easier way to make a living," I said to Vinny one day.

"Like how?"

"Like selling the cars instead of delivering them to the rental places." I'd come to realize that no one knew where the cars were at any given time. The paperwork was shoddy at best, and we often just dropped cars in parking lots, picked up new ones, and continued on our way, without signing anything.

Vinny's jaw dropped. "Are you out of your friggin' mind? We'll get caught."

"I doubt it."

I took out an ad in the local *Pennysaver*, advertising slightly used cars for sale. We undercut their Blue Book value by 25 percent. The phone rang off the hook. But this time, I wasn't stupid. I ran the scam for a month, pocketed a pile of money, and quit. Most thieves get caught because they're greedy, a character flaw I'd left behind at MCC.

❊　❊　❊

We were living off our ill-gotten gains and doing rather nicely. I was contemplating a move back to New York. I missed my family. Before I had a chance to talk to Vinny about it, I got a call from my father.

"Your mother died, Terri."

I certainly wasn't shocked. She'd been in and out of hospitals for a while, mostly for acute alcoholism. During one of her stays, she had a nurse come to *Bill Bailey's* and pick up a six-pack of beer every day. I gave it to her because I knew that if I didn't, she'd go elsewhere and have to pay for it. My mother had a disease, which I'd inherited, and I certainly hoped that I didn't end up like her.

I flew to New York for the funeral, but instead of staying, I brought my father back to Miami with me. He was eighty-four, still feisty, but beginning to slow down. His empire was being chipped away by young Turks from the Genovese family, and he didn't much care. He wanted to live out his years in relative peace. Enough was enough.

I rented a house for him not far from where Vinny and I were living. He was bait for the numerous widows who inhabit Florida. They took one look at the still-handsome Italian and babied him like mother hens. He loved every second of it. He ate at a different woman's house every day. He'd get up in the morning and consult his address book. "Let's see," he'd muse, "who's gonna be my Yenta-of-the-Day?"

One day, while on his way to the beach, he slipped and broke his hip. My father thought that he was thirty-five and tried to play the part, jogging in the sand when he should have been shuffling like the rest of the one-foot-in-the-grave octogenarians. After he was released from the hospital, he was relegated to using a walker. He grumbled and moaned, but he got used to it. He got even more attention from the old ladies.

I was now running back and forth between two households, making certain that my father was okay and caring for Vinny and me. A little taxing, but since I wasn't working, I was able to handle it. Vinny spent his days at the track, and he was managing to keep his head above water and make a little money gambling.

One day he came home clutching what looked like a bottle of detergent.

"Check this out," he said, and put the bottle on the coffee table in the living room.

A bottle of laundry soap, big deal. I told him so.

"Look closer," he said.

I did. The white stuff inside the bottle wasn't soap. It was cocaine. There had to be a pound of the stuff.

"Where'd you get this crap?"

"Guy lost a bet, big time. Want some? I'll sell what we don't use."

I never tried coke in my life, never had the desire. The people that I'd seen on it were constantly babbling, staying up for days on end, not eating. It had no allure for me, and I'd always resisted when it was offered.

"No thanks."

"Come on," Vinny insisted, "it's good shit. Enhances your personality."

"What happens if you're an asshole?" I said.

He caught the dig and said, "Don't be a wiseguy. Try some, it's great shit, one hundred percent pure."

I'd like to say that he wore me down, but truthfully, I had been straight for a long time and wanted a rush. I was an addict, and once an addict....

We proceeded to run through about an ounce. That's a lot of coke. I lost track of time, but we probably stayed up for at least two days, maybe three, and didn't eat anything during the entire period. It was fun for a while, but after being deprived of sleep and food for that long, my body began to break down. I got the shakes, began sweating profusely, and my heart started to race. I was no longer having a good time. I was scared, thinking that my chest was going to explode.

"Vinny, I need something to bring me down," I said breathlessly.

He searched the house for booze, but we'd drunk it all. It was two o'clock in the morning; liquor stores were closed.

I really thought I was going to die and began to cry. Vinny panicked.

"I got something," he said and vanished into the bedroom. He came out with a dime bag of heroin.

I was about to become hooked again. Vinny had obviously been shooting without my knowledge. He was very good at hiding his addiction.

✳ ✳ ✳

I was mainlining within a week, hopelessly hooked within two. It was hot in Florida, and my arms were exposed, so I took to shooting in areas that weren't readily visible, like behind my knees or between my toes. After a while, I got really lazy and began shooting up between my fingers because I didn't want to bend down. A week after I started doing the finger thing, I noticed that the web of the skin between the second and third fingers of my left hand was becoming inflamed. I dismissed the swelling and pain; the only thing I was concerned about was where I was going to get my next fix. Vinny was no help. He'd been dabbling in heroin for years and now, because he no longer had to sneak shots, was a full-fledged junkie. It takes one to know one.

My hand got worse, swelling to the size of a catcher's mitt. I knew I had a problem and could put off a trip to the emergency room no longer.

I was examined and x-rayed, the diagnosis being a severe infection and the beginnings of gangrene brought on by shooting with an infected needle. I was told I had to have the hand amputated or risk dying.

No way I was going to do either. I decided to fly

back to New York to see a specialist. I was on a plane the next day, high on painkillers and a double dime bag to alleviate the pain.

A specialist at Staten Island Hospital told me that I might lose my arm up to my elbow unless I agreed to an experimental procedure.

"Doctor," I said, delirious with pain and medication, "do anything that you think is right. I'm left-handed, hate to have to learn to be a righty at my age."

I underwent a surgical procedure to clean out the wound. My middle finger was in bad shape, shriveled and rapidly turning black. The surgeon opened my abdomen and sewed the finger into the folds of skin, hoping that healthy tissue from my belly would graft naturally to my infected finger.

For three of the most painful weeks I can remember, I lay in a hospital bed with minimal painkillers, because it affected the grafting process, and screaming out in agony every time I moved and pulled on the stitches. But the graft took; I was going to be fine.

Vinny called from Miami every day. He was either high or in need of a fix. I felt sorry for him, and worse, sorrier for myself. I'd had it with Vinny Mirabile, booze, drugs, and my lifestyle. It turned out that my infection was the best thing that ever happened to me. I learned my lesson; I was finally going to quit abusing myself for good.

"When are you coming home, Baby?" Vinny asked one day, his withdrawal symptoms evident despite the miles that separated us. He needed a fix.

"I'm not, Vinny. We're through."

Momentary silence while my news flash soaked in. "Through? Us? Aw, c'mon, Terri, we—"

I hung up on him.

❋ ❋ ❋

I checked myself into Bailey Seton Hospital on Staten Island, a well-known drug treatment facility, in March 1988. I did my ninety days, determined to beat the smack. But I had been determined before, only to slide back into addiction. Being aware that I was weak and couldn't rely on a treatment program alone made me all the more committed to beat this thing once and for all.

I was released from the program feeling run down, but upbeat. I'd sooner commit suicide than go back to drugs. I bought a revolver on the street to use on myself if I ever went near heroin again. I never did, and thirteen years later, I'm still clean. A happy ending? Hardly.

I went back to Florida to get my father and moved him back to his old house. He was happy but frail, his days as a crime kingpin behind him. His younger brothers, Mike and Pope, still kept their hand in the family business, but for the most part, the Dalessio criminal empire had faded into oblivion.

I got a good job running a big motel on Staten Island. It was owned by a conglomerate from California, and they treated me well. I had a company car–a cute little Mustang–and ran the place like it was my own business.

My sons were productive citizens, surprising, considering their environment. Ronnie was engaged to be married, and both he and his brother, Frankie, were union tile mechanics, making decent livings. They had just completed a job refinishing the Museum of Natural History with a new tile facade and were flush with money. They decided to flee the city and bought houses within four miles of each other in the Pocono Mountains in Pennsylvania. I gave them each $3,000 toward the purchase of their homes. Frankie was engaged shortly thereafter and today, each has four kids. They're still neighbors and best friends.

John, my son that Chin's family had babied and spoiled, was on his second tour of duty as a navy SEAL. My other son, Lenny, didn't fit the Dee mold. He was very handsome, but not in the rugged way that was the norm for the males of my family. His looks were delicate, his manner more refined. While his brothers were into outdoor activities, Lenny gravitated toward the arts. His college degree was in horticulture. It came as no surprise to our family that he came out as gay when he was twenty years old. It made little difference to me; he was my son and I loved him. My father and uncles, contrary to what you might expect from macho Italian types, embraced him as a Dee and loved him for who he was.

※   ※   ※

I continued at the motel for about a year. One day, as I was leaving the office, I slipped on a wet patch of asphalt and severely injured my back, further aggravating the discs I'd injured when I fell in my bar fifteen years earlier. I was in the hospital for two weeks. I was diagnosed with pulled tendons and ligaments and a ruptured disc. Again, my doctor recommended surgery, and once again, I refused, only this time I didn't revert to heroin as a pain reliever. Fortunately, I was ambulatory and didn't have the severe pain I'd had as a result of the first fall, but I was very uncomfortable. Unable to work, I was placed on compensation, where I remain today.

Between the money I'd saved and the compensation, I was able to survive. At fifty-four a new career didn't hold much allure. I wanted to enjoy my grand-children and grow old with grace and style.

❋ ❋ ❋

Three years passed. I could honestly say that I was no longer tempted by drugs. My junkie friends had given up trying to have me rejoin the party. Vinny Mirabile called occasionally, trying to entice me back to Florida and the partying lifestyle. He never straightened out and today still chases the next shot. Some of my friends wised up and went for the cure, others OD'd, some, in their sixties like Vinny, are still using.

One of the survivors was Ann Forney. Ann was a hard-core user who saw the light at about the same time I did. We were never really close during the needle days. Junkies don't form lasting relation-ships. Our was a friendship born out of desperation: mutual connections, communal shooting galleries, and shared needles. Your buddy remained a buddy as long as he or she could facilitate your high and empathize when your dealer got busted.

Ann and I became good friends when we kicked our habits. We needed each other as much for moral support as we did to share "girl" things. Booze and drugs weren't part of our lives anymore. We under-stood that friendship meant more than helping your pal tie off a vein.

We did normal things: shopping, going to the movies, bragging about the grandkids. Life was good. Then one day, we were walking past Bailey Seton Hospital, and the pain of our former lifestyles came flooding back.

"Seems like a million years ago," Ann said. She was my age, fifty-six, but looked older, having used heroin for twenty-five years.

"Four years, Ann," I said, but she was right, it was another lifetime.

It was mid-November. We were on our way to the ferry to invade Manhattan to do some Christmas shopping before the rush after Thanksgiving. We shrugged off the bad years and continued walking.

Ann grabbed my arm. "Terri, look."

A banner strung above the hospital entrance read: Free AIDS Testing.

"Have you ever been tested?" I asked.

She shook her head. "You?"

"No."

We decided to take the test. It was free, and we had forty minutes to kill before the next ferry left for the Battery. I had no fear about the results. I'd never felt better in my life. I was training at a local gym, eating right, and sleeping like the proverbial baby.

Ann claimed no symptoms, either. I had noticed, however, that she seemed to be losing some hair. There were always long strands covering her clothing.

"Cats," she told me. Indeed, she had seven of them.

We had blood drawn and proceeded to the boat. I gave no further thought to the possibility of AIDS.

❋　❋　❋

I received a letter two weeks later asking me to call for an appointment to discuss my test results. I felt a moment of panic and called Ann.

"Don't worry about it," she said. "We're former patients. This is the way it's done."

"Did you go?"

"Yesterday. They give you a clean bill, then lecture you for five minutes about staying off drugs and having safe sex. I hadda giggle. Last time I had sex, if I can remember that long ago, it was safe because my boyfriend's wife was out of town."

We laughed, promised to get together for lunch at the end of the week, and hung up. Ann had tried to reassure me, but I wasn't totally convinced.

I called for my appointment, trying to read something into the way the secretary responded to me. She sounded normal, and she had my results, didn't she? With all my street smarts, I couldn't detect emotion in her voice, which undoubtedly would have been evident had she been talking to a dead woman. I decompressed a little, got a good night's sleep, and was thirty minutes early for my appointment the next day.

✻ ✻ ✻

A young doctor breezed into the examining room. The first words out of his mouth were, "Did you bring anyone with you today?"

"Now why would I want to do that?" The words were catching in my throat.

He looked uneasy, couldn't meet my gaze.

"Well, uh...usually it's a good idea to have a family member or someone present, you know...."

"No, I don't know," I said, but I did.

He sighed. "You're HIV positive. I'm sorry."

He was sorry? He had no idea what sorry was.

✻ ✻ ✻

1992. AIDS was a killer, and I was full blown. The drugs that extend life today weren't around back then. AZT, the wonder drug of the day, was just being introduced, and its long-term effects weren't known. To my way of thinking, I had just been given a death sentence. I couldn't believe it. I felt fine.

I was in a fog for the rest of my visit. The doctor had his nurse make a series of appointments for me so I could begin treatment. I felt much the same as I did when Tommy Ernst and Vinny Rizzo were murdered: detached, unhinged, depressed. People were talking to me, and I pretended to pay attention to what they were saying, but I felt as if they were shouting to me from the end of a very long tunnel.

I left the hospital clutching a bunch of papers and drug-protocol forms.

The first thing I did when I got home was call Ann. I told her the bad news. She took it a lot better than I expected.

"I'm so sorry, Terri," she said in a monotone. At the time, I thought it was from her shock at hearing the news and feeling guilty that I was sick and she wasn't. A few years later, I found out that Ann's test had been positive, too. For some unexplained reason, she wanted to keep it a secret. She hid the disease from everyone for years until the ravages of her illness became evident. She died in November 2001.

My treatment was to begin in a week. I wasn't as frightened about my condition as I was about telling my family. Another sit-down that I wasn't looking forward to. I decided to tell my kids, no one else. They would never think that I'd have worse news than when I told them that I was going to jail, but in my life, there was always room for another disaster.

I spared my father. He went to his grave never knowing that I had AIDS.

❀ ❀ ❀

I called John first. Despite being the baby, he was the toughest of the lot. He didn't handle the news well. He took an emergency leave from the navy and was on a plane home the next day. That day, at my apartment, Ronnie and Frank accepted my announcement with stunned disbelief. Lenny seemed as if he was in another world. He hung back when his brothers left.

"Mom," he said, "I've got something to tell you."

"What, honey?"

He lowered his eyes. "I've got it, too. I've got AIDS."

The news hit me with such force that I felt like I was going to faint. I staggered back to the sofa and fell onto it. There's no news so devastating as learning that one of your children has a fatal illness. From that moment, I stopped feeling sorry for myself and focused all my love and energy on Lenny.

I got up, went to him. We hugged each other and cried. Finally I said, "How bad?"

"Full blown. I've had it for a year. No one knows."

"Your brothers?"

He shook his head. "No one."

"Why didn't you tell me, at least?"

He snorted. "What for? So you could worry yourself into an early grave? Now you have to know."

"What treatment–?"

He held up a hand. "None, Mom. I'm not taking anything."

"What!" I was incredulous. "You've got your whole life–"

"What life!" he shouted at me. "I'm not going to waste away, be a burden on my family. I don't want to linger," he said softly. He led me to the sofa, and we both sat. "You know the Hemlock Society?"

I shook my head.

"They help you die, Mom. I'm gonna do it. I've made up my mind."

Lenny had always been very vain, even as a kid. He was proud of his good looks and worked hard to stay in shape. The thought of wasting away was probably devastating to him.

We talked for hours. Well, he talked, I pleaded. I wanted my son with me for every possible second, and the thought that he'd allow himself to die, or have someone assist him in killing himself, petrified me. Finally, we came to an agreement. Presently, he looked fine, felt good. The first time he saw himself deteriorating or felt he was becoming a burden, he'd call the Hemlock Society and put himself in its hands. He would also begin medical treatment.

Lenny was no longer a child. He had the right to decide his own future, but I hoped that he'd be one of the few who survived when others with AIDS lost the fight. There were also great medical inroads being made in combating the disease. Perhaps Lenny would be a lucky recipient of a miracle drug. As for myself, my survival instinct had kicked in. If this thing was going to kill me, I'd go down fighting.

❋ ❋ ❋

I began my treatment. I was given AZT and DDI, their pharmaceutical names too complicated to pronounce. Two pills each, twice daily. I was taking the medications for about a week when the first side effects appeared. I was told to expect tiredness, perhaps nausea. What I got was an allergic reaction. I couldn't breathe, and my body swelled up like someone pumped me full of helium. I was taken off those drugs and put on Zerit and Epizir. They seemed to work and initially. I experienced no side effects or symptoms of the disease.

I maintained my health for about a year before I began to get very sick. I would be hospitalized more than forty times over the next eight years, mostly suffering from pneumonia, which I was able to handle both physically and mentally. I got it, went into the hospital, got rid of it, came out. What I wasn't prepared for was a yearlong bout with peripheral neuropathy, a devastating nerve disease brought on by the AIDS medication.

I was in my apartment one evening, peeling potatoes for dinner, when the index finger of my right hand suddenly shot straight into the air. It was stiff as a board; I couldn't lower it. Then my toes did the same thing. Before long, I was completely crippled, confined to bed or a wheelchair, unable to walk. One of the symptoms of the disease is that my feet got extremely hot, like they were on fire. It was torture until they changed my prescriptions to two new medications, Viracett (which I subsequently stopped taking) and Vired, which I'm still on.

I stabilized and began to feel much better. I still occasionally come down with pneumonia or a mild viral infection, but otherwise, I remain fairly healthy. I take one day at a time.

There's nothing like countless brushes with death to make a person see life differently. I had no idea how much longer I'd be around, and there were two things I wanted to do before I died. One was to give my kids what money I could afford to give them. I had some savings and gave $40,000 to my boys.

The second thing I wanted to do was find the daughter I'd given up for adoption. I refused to die until I located her.

14 The Slow Climb Back

I didn't know where to begin. Initially, I checked with the New York Foundling Hospital where my daughter Karen Ruth was born. I was told that they couldn't release any information unless my daughter came looking for *me*, and the odds of that happening after all these years was infinitesimal. If she had a burning desire to find her birth mother, I didn't think she would have waited thirty-two years. But I held out hope.

I contacted a private investigator who did occasional work for the mob doing wiretap sweeps. He suggested that I call as many foundling hospitals as I could find and leave my name on the chance that Karen might be looking for me. I called more than seventy hospitals that specialized in caring for unwed mothers and orphans. Then I waited. I fantasized about what her life might be like, hoping that it didn't turn out to be anything like mine.

Weeks passed. Months. Karen hadn't initiated contact, but that didn't surprise me. I was disappointed, but not discouraged. I believed that someday she would reach out to me. While I was waiting for that to happen, I had to concentrate on surviving.

I took my medication religiously, never missed a doctor's appointment, and for the first time in a long time, I was treating my body with respect: no alcohol, definitely no drugs, and I was only eating food that was good for me. Depriving myself of pizza was almost like withdrawing from heroin.

Lenny seemed to be doing well, too. He was taking his prescribed drugs and was mostly in good spirits. I heard no more talk of calling the ghouls from the Hemlock Society.

❊ ❊ ❊

I decided to move from Staten Island. Too many bad memories. I felt a change would be good for me, but I still wanted to remain within striking distance of the city. Once a New Yorker, always a New Yorker.

I scanned the real estate ads in the Northern New Jersey newspapers and found several available apartments and condos right across the Hudson. I settled on a studio apartment in a condominium in the bedroom community of Old Bridge, primarily because, according to the real estate agent, it was owned by two former policewomen who lived in the downstairs apartment. What straighter, more stable landlords could there be than two former cops? I also took it because I had limited funds and the rent was right. I moved in July 1993, without ever meeting the landlords. Next time, I'll know better.

The condo was owned by two former policewomen all right, but the real estate agent failed to mention, either by design or ignorance, that both were lesbians and hard-core heroin and Percocet addicts. Percocet, for the uninitiated, is a powerful painkiller. I was hard pressed to imagine anyone taking it along with heroin. A deadly combination, for sure. A slight overdose could stop the heart of a rutting water buffalo.

Diane and Lucille had been with the NYPD. Diane was a cute blonde, slim, with short hair, in her early thirties. She'd been injured in an undercover operation and retired on a disability pension. Lucille, about the same age, looked like Hulk Hogan with breasts. She, too, was out on a disability pension.

As soon as we laid eyes on each other, we recognized each other as junkies. Fortunately, I was of the recovering variety; Diane and Lucille were still using, heavily. While I didn't want to be around heroin, I felt insulated enough in my apartment where I wouldn't be tempted. Besides, their lifestyle precluded straight women. We did, however, talk occasionally, and they weren't shy about how they existed from day to day.

Both women had good (tax-free) pensions, but their monthly checks didn't nearly cover their drug expenses. In addition to shooting numerous bags of smack a day, they had the most voracious appetite for Percocet I'd ever seen. They popped percs like they were M&Ms. To supplement their income, they would rip off local supermarkets. These were two of the ballsiest people I've ever run across. In my wildest days, I would never have considered doing what these two crazies were doing routinely.

In addition to dealing to anyone who would buy from them (Diane: "If I can't spot an undercover cop by this time, I might as well lock *myself* up"), both would go to a supermarket, take separate carts, and proceed to fill them with high-priced items, like expensive cuts of meat, exotic seafood, and cigarettes. With the carts overflowing, they would saunter right out the front door without paying. After they loaded their van, they'd make stops at area restaurants, bars, and candy stores and peddle the swag for half the wholesale price. They'd do this on a daily basis, often returning to the same super-market two or three times a week.

I tried to steer clear of them, but the inevitable meetings in front of the condo sent chills through my body. I could see that they were both on the road to ruin, as I had been just a few years before. The thought that I could slip back into the lifestyle scared the hell out of me. I avoided them like they had a disease, which, in a manner of speaking, they did.

❋　❋　❋

My cache of funds was diminishing. I needed work. I knew enough to stay clear of the bar business, but wanted something a little challenging to occupy my mind. I made some calls to friends and family, put out the word that I was seeking employment, sat back, and waited.

One (probably the only) good thing about being involved in our world was that the mob knew how to network. I think they invented the word. Within hours, the phone was ringing off the hook. Most of the jobs offered, however, involved some sort of criminal activity. Running wire rooms, managing whorehouses, and laundering money was not exact-ly my idea of a good career move. Eventually I got a call from an old acquaintance who extended a job offer that wouldn't get me three-to-five in MCC.

Clem, the wiseguy who had driven me to my his-toric sit-down with Jimmy Red and supplied the gun I wanted to use on low-level street punk Frank Guzzio, phoned and told me he had gone legit, opened up a moving business, and needed an office manager.

"Moving business?" I said. "What're you moving? Guns?"

He seemed offended, shifty as ever, but visibly insulted. "It's a legit business, wise-ass. You wanna run the office or not?"

The "office" turned out to be the basement of his mother's house in Bensonhurst. Clem's idea of a "legitimate" business was an uninsured, unlicensed, run-by-the-seat-of-your-pants operation that paid no taxes, hired illegal aliens, and found it a good business practice to write accounts receivable on beer coasters.

I accepted the job and took the place over. Within a month, I had the business–Half Price Movers–paying taxes and keeping a decent set of books. The illegals stayed. For the discount rates Clem was charging, and the subsequent salaries he was paying, I was surprised that he was able to get *any* employees, illegal or otherwise.

I wasn't too pleased with my salary, either. He was paying me $200 a week cash, off-the-books slave wages for what I was doing. I was literally running the business. After two months, Clem never even bothered to come to the office anymore. He didn't need to waste his time making an honest dollar with me running his operation; now he could devote his time to gun running, drug dealing, and petty thievery. No matter how much clean money there was to be made, a wiseguy didn't feel whole unless he was bringing in some dirty cash. He'd call several times a day to see how things were going.

"I'll tell you how things are going," I said. "I quit."

He panicked. Not only had I straightened out his business, but I had created a small advertising budget, and we were beginning to get decent clients, not the typical Clem client: shylock victims looking to make a midnight move before they had their legs broken for nonpayment of loans.

We went into arbitration. I wanted more money, and Clem, the cheap bastard, didn't want to part with it. Finally, we came to an agreement. At the end of a year, if business was still good, he'd make me an equal partner.

"Put it on paper," I said.

"Done."

❅ ❅ ❅

A year flew by. My health was status quo. I felt fine; my T-cell count, the holy grail of AIDS sufferers, was high.

Business was better than ever. Prior to me invoking the partnership agreement, I told Clem that we needed more office space.

"How's about we expand to the garage?" he said. A regular Donald Trump.

"Okay, forget moving. We need to see a lawyer by the end of the month."

"What for?"

"The year's up." I said. "Business is great. We have an agreement."

"Oh," Clem said, "I wanna talk to you about that."

The sonofabitch was going to renege, I felt it.

"I don't think I can do that," he said. "You know how it is."

"No," I said, my anger rising, "how is it?"

Clem babbled for twenty minutes about how sick his mother was, how his back hurt him, that his girlfriend was pregnant, every excuse imaginable that had absolutely nothing to do with the fact that he was shutting me out. The contract we had wasn't worth the paper it was written on. Try suing someone who didn't have a bank account, own a house or a car, and had the business in his eighty-five year-old mother's name.

In the not-too-distant past, Little Tiger would have gotten a sawed-off shotgun and used it as a collective bargaining tool. But now I was Paper Tiger, tired of the violence, deceit, and backstabbing that is inherent in the "new" mob.

The gangsters of my father's era had a sense of honor; their word was their bond. Clem wasn't an aberration in today's world of wiseguys. What was once a loyal society has degenerated into the turncoat Mafia we read about almost daily in the newspapers. The mob is killing itself off with less-than-dependable people who would sooner turn in their comrades than suffer the consequences of their lifestyles. And then there's the Clems of our world who cheat and lie to anyone as easily as they draw a breath.

I was tired of arguing.

"You know, Clem, keep your goddamn business. I'm gone. In a year, you won't have a business. You're too stupid and selfish to run it."

I was fifty-eight years old, sick, with no money and no future. What else could go wrong?

❋ ❋ ❋

I had my mother's jewelry locked in a strongbox in my apartment in Old Bridge. It was worth about $35,000, and while I needed the money, I couldn't bring myself to pawn it. It was part of our history, when the Dees were a formidable presence on Staten Island and my father lavished gifts upon my mother. I considered them the good old days; we all have them.

I'd take the jewelry out occasionally, examine some of the intricate pieces, and reminisce about how beautiful my mother looked when she wore them, before the ravages of alcohol ripped her looks to shreds.

I went directly home the afternoon that Clem and I had our big blowout. I wanted to look at the jewelry, caress the gold and precious stones, propel myself back to a happier time.

I entered a ransacked apartment. Of course the strongbox was gone, the heirloom jewelry along with it.

I immediately suspected my junkie landlords, Diane and Lucille. I called the police, went downstairs, and knocked on their door. As soon as Diane swung open the screen, I knew she'd done it. I've been on the street too long to mistake the body language. Before I said anything, her movements became defensive, protective.

I never bothered to confront her. What was the use? I know junkies, and junkies never tell the truth. What was I going to do, beat a confession out of her? I was destroyed, demoralized, and defeated. I just didn't give a damn.

The cops came and went. My apartment was coated with a fine layer of fingerprint powder. Diane's prints were all over the apartment, as were Lucille's. And why shouldn't they be? They owned the condo. The investigation went nowhere. I moved back to Staten Island.

❋　❋　❋

Since I was considered totally disabled, I began drawing a small monthly check from Social Security. I was too ashamed to ask my father for any money. Besides, he wasn't that well off anymore. As his empire dried up and legal bills mounted, his supply of cash dried up, too. During the 1970s and 1980s, the government had been relentless in dogging the Dees with grand jury investigations and a flood of subpoenas. You'd be surprised how fast cash reserves get eaten up when $400-an-hour lawyers start to feed on it.

At least I had my boys. Lenny was my biggest concern, but he seemed to be holding his own. I hadn't heard any talk about the Hemlock Society for months, and while he'd had one bout with pneumonia, he seemed to be in good spirits.

He stopped by one day, and we talked for a few hours. I made us lunch. Everything seemed normal except for the extra-long hug I got as he was leaving. A bolt of dread shot through me.

I held him by the shoulders, looked him squarely in the eyes.

"Everything okay?"

He smiled wanly, but returned my gaze. "Yeah, Ma, sure."

There was nothing hidden behind his expression that suggested anything different. I had no choice but to believe him. I wanted to believe him.

"You'd tell me if you're thinking of those Morlock—"

He smiled. "Hemlock, Mom."

"Yeah, whatever. Those people. You're not considering doing anything foolish, are you?"

He hesitated for a moment. "Foolish? Not me, Mom. Nothing foolish."

"Why don't you stay here tonight, Lenny? Tomorrow we can go over to Grandpa's. He'd like to see you." I wanted to keep him close by me. I had a feeling of dread.

He begged off. Maybe the next day, he told me.

I went to bed with an ache in my chest. Parents

know their kids, mothers most of all. He was hiding something from me.

Two days later, a doctor called me from St. Vincent's Hospital in Manhattan. Lenny had been admitted with congestive heart failure the evening before. He had died in his sleep.

My legs felt rubbery as I sought out a chair. "Why wasn't I notified?" I barely managed to get the words out.

"He had no identification, ma'am. Two men brought him to the ER in a semicoma."

"So how did you get my number?"

He sighed. "When your son passed away, one of the men who brought him in gave me a piece of paper with your name and number."

"Where is this person now—the one who gave you my number?"

"Gone. Took off, both of them. We have no idea who they were."

❊ ❊ ❊

Three days after the funeral, I got a Mass card from the Hemlock Society. I pretty much figured out that Lenny had, indeed, gone to them, and whatever they gave my son, it mimicked or caused heart failure. I didn't authorize an autopsy. He was such a beautiful boy; I didn't want to see him cut up.

I decided after I'd returned home from the cemetery that I was going to kill myself. The revolver I'd bought to use if I ever went back on heroin was wrapped in a towel and secreted behind the boiler in the basement of my father's house. I retrieved it that night and brought it home.

It took me two hours to compose a letter to my kids. In it, I asked forgiveness and explained that I couldn't go on knowing that I might have done something to have kept Lenny home with me that night. I realize now that I was irrational. He was going to take his own life regardless of what I tried to do to stop him. At the time, however, I blamed myself for his death. I was also tired of struggling. I realized how Lenny must have felt when he said that he didn't want to be a burden to anyone.

I had planned on drinking as much Scotch as I could force into my body before I pulled the trigger, but now that the time was near, I didn't want to go out high. At least I was beyond that.

Women don't generally shoot themselves. The preferred method is an overdose of pills or gas, but I was a Dee, most certainly not a wimp. As I put the barrel of the gun in my mouth I wondered what my father would think. Morbidly, I thought he'd give me credit for taking the man's way out. After all, I was his Little Tiger.

I pulled back the hammer, tasting the cool metal, tinged with the bitterness of gun oil. Vain to the end, I decided that I didn't want someone to find me minus the back of my head, so I lowered the pistol to my chest.

I held it there for what seemed like hours. A three-pound, single-action trigger pull. If I sneezed, it would fire. I had no conscious thoughts of *not* doing it. I wasn't scared. After a while, I looked down and saw my hand lowering as if by some mysterious force. *I wanted to shoot myself.* Why couldn't I do it?

I placed the gun on the living-room floor, got up, and went to bed. No tears, no relief, just confusion. It was as if the act of attempting suicide was all I needed. Or was I being spared for something else?

❋   ❋   ❋

When I got up the next day, I felt better. I had an appetite for the first time in days. As I prepared breakfast, I thought back on the events of the night before. What the hell had made me stop?

The phone rang.

"Hello," I said, sounding surprisingly cheery.

"Is this Theresa Dalessio?" a youthful female voice said.

"Yes. Who is this?"

"My name's Phyllis Mackie, Ms. Dalessio. I work at the New York Foundling Hospital."

My knees got weak. I felt faint. I found a chair.

"Ms. Dalessio? Are you there?"

"Yes," I squeaked, "I'm here."

"We've been contacted by Stephanie Grasso. She–"

"Who?"

"Your daughter, ma'am."

"My daughter's name is Karen. I don't know–"

"Ma'am, are you sitting down? It might be better if you sat down."

"Yes, yes, I feel weak. I am sitting. Could you please tell me what's going on?"

She explained that it was the hospital's policy that whenever a child or birth mother initiates contact, that the administration check with the other party before releasing a phone number.

"Do you want to talk to your daughter, ma'am?"

I broke down in a flood of tears.

I told her that it sounded like a very good idea.

Epilogue

My daughter had recently discovered that she was pregnant and decided that she wanted her baby to know who her grandmother was. She had contacted an adoption registry service, and they found me in less than a week.

We talked on the phone for two hours, both desperate to know as much about each other as we could jam into a phone conversation. I apologized for giving her up, but what happened thirty-seven years ago was of no consequence for her. She wanted to know her mother, that's all she cared about.

Her adoptive parents had named her Stephanie. I adjusted to the sound of it. Within twenty minutes, the name Stephanie rolled off my tongue like I'd been saying it all my life. She was raised in New Jersey and had married a Long Branch, New Jersey, police officer. She lived less than thirty minutes away from my Old Bridge condo and directly across the Goethals Bridge from Staten Island. Not a story that would captivate fans of *Unsolved Mysteries*, but interesting, nonetheless.

We agreed to meet at her home the next day. Once again I had important news to tell my sons. It seemed that every time I called them lately, I had some earth-shattering information to impart. I knew that they would accept Stephanie's existence with great enthusiasm. My father would be another story. He was the reason she was put up for adoption in the first place.

In my entire life, I can't remember ever fearing my father. The day I marched into his home to tell him about my daughter was the first time I felt real dread.

My father was eighty-five and had just suffered a minor stroke. He was confined to a wheelchair and spent his days reading or watching old movies on TV. His mind was still sharp, and when I went to the house that day, he knew I didn't stop by just to say hello.

I told him about Stephanie. He looked at me for a few moments, the old lion about to share the wisdom of the Dees with his Little Tiger.

Tears came to his eyes, and he held his arms out to me. We held each other, sobbing like little kids.

"This is wonderful news, Tiger. You really should have told me about her before this."

I raised my eyebrows. "C'mon, Dad. I valued my life."

He laughed. "Age mellows everybody, Tiger, even us Dees. If Al Capone would have lived to be an old man, he would've spent his last years baking cookies." He sipped from a glass of red wine. "So when do I get to see my granddaughter?"

"Tomorrow."

I stayed with my father a few more hours. I can't remember when I enjoyed or valued his company more.

❋ ❋ ❋

The reunion was heart wrenching. We couldn't let go of each other. Stephanie's husband, a big bear of a guy, felt like a fifth wheel, but he watched us, beaming. His wife was happy, and that's all he seemed to care about.

We met my father, Frank, and Ronnie at my father's house on Staten Island. John was in Europe, whereabouts unknown. I'd called the Department of the Navy, but couldn't get anything out of them. He was still with the SEALs. Since there was no family emergency, I guess that explained their reluctance to give me any information.

That afternoon was the happiest of my life, and I'm positive that I owe my longevity to the harmony that I finally achieved that day. We were a family once again.

I relocated to a small apartment, where I remain today, leased through the Division of AIDS Services. Ironically, it's in Alphabet City, whose streets I prowled only a few years earlier in search of my next fix. The neighborhood has become gentrified, the streets devoid of junkies.

My father died in 1995, I believe a happy man. My Uncle Mike is gone; my Uncle Pope, at eighty-nine, is the last of the notorious Dee brothers. He lives quietly with his girlfriend on Staten Island. My daughter and sons are doing well; we visit often. Sadly, my son John, the navy SEAL, who never had a drink or smoked a cigarette in his life and ran five miles a day, died of a heart attack while watching television. He was thirty-six.

Anyone who lived the sort of life I led and says that they have no regrets is a liar. Still, I hear that all the time. A lot of ex-cons, junkies, and other miscreants I know say that if they had it to do all over again, they'd do it the same way because it was a helluva ride.

I can agree with the wild-ride part, but the only portion of my life that I'd want to relive is my youth. My happiest moments were living those good years when my mother was sober, my family was cohesive, when gangsters were shooting each other instead of their mouths, and when a person's word was everything.

But what I'd really love to experience over and over again would be the days when my father would come home, hug me, and say, "C'mon, Tiger, let's make the rounds."

Index

Index

Index

Index